# PERSONAL DISCOVERY
# FOR WOMEN

## A PRACTICAL GUIDE TO DISCOVERING AND FULFILLING YOUR UNIQUE PURPOSE

### OMOKOREDE FASORO

WESTBOW
PRESS®
A DIVISION OF THOMAS NELSON
& ZONDERVAN

WestBow Press books may be ordered through booksellers or by contacting:

WestBow Press
A Division of Thomas Nelson & Zondervan
1663 Liberty Drive
Bloomington, IN 47403
www.westbowpress.com
844-714-3454

Scripture quotations taken from The Holy Bible, New International Version® NIV® Copyright © 1973 1978 1984 2011 by Biblica, Inc. TM. Used by permission. All rights reserved worldwide.

Scripture taken from the New King James Version® Copyright © 1982 by Thomas Nelson. Used by permission. All rights reserved.

ISBN: 978-1-6642-4251-7 (sc)
ISBN: 978-1-6642-4252-4 (hc)
ISBN: 978-1-6642-4250-0 (e)

Library of Congress Control Number: 2021916203

Print information available on the last page.

WestBow Press rev. date: 11/05/2021

# DEDICATION

This book is dedicated to every woman who has a desire
to find her true self and to make an impact on her generation.

# CONTENTS

# ENDORSEMENTS FOR PERSONAL DISCOVERY FOR WOMEN

What a blessing to have a book just for me…a woman! I have needed help for discovering and fulfilling my purpose throughout my life and to know how to make a difference in my life and the generations after me. This excellent book will show you: How to be relevant and to make an impact in your life. Omokorede shows how we can discover who we are – that enormous question that never seems to be answered. But in this book, it is! God is the One who has created us and given us His purpose and part of that purpose is discovering God's original intention and plan for our lives. She gives exact and practical ways to discern your passions and desires for your life. You don't want to miss this exceptional book!

**Lane P. Jordan is the best-selling author of *12 Steps to Becoming a More Organized Woman*, as well as four other books; international motivational and inspirational speaker, professional life coach; Bible teacher; singer and artist.**

The pertinent question about how a woman can fulfill purpose and live a meaningful life is answered in this book - *Personal Discovery for Women* - written by Omokorede Fasoro.

Omokorede - a Personal Discovery Coach with close to 20 years' experience as a professional trainer in various capacities and at different levels, most especially in the areas of personal discovery, self-development, and entrepreneurship, shares from her wealth of experience both professionally and in the ministry, the steps to take in the journey to personal discovery, in order to live a life of impact.

Using her personal experiences and those learnt from others, she unveils the five petals of personal discovery amongst other things, which lead to self-fulfillment and realization of self-worth. This book is a must read for every woman who wishes to live a purpose-driven life.

**Funmilayo Arowoogun - (FIAM, FIMC) President, NECA's Network of Entrepreneurial Women, Nigeria.**


Whether we are aware of it or not, we are all on a journey through this life, where we seek to discover the answer to two questions:

1. Who am I?
2. What was I put on this earth to do?

Omokorede Fasoro in her new book titled *Personal Discovery for Women*, provides practical guidelines for every woman to answer these all-important questions. Her vulnerability and practical insights make this book a must read for every woman.

**Bola Olawale, Publisher *Gem Woman Magazine*, Convener BSS Women Conferences.**

Congratulations to every woman who will read this amazing, detailed book on PERSONAL DISCOVERY, which for me is simply how to come out of your dark times or wilderness period by getting rid of limiting beliefs and going on to become an amazement to your world.

Woman, there is more to life than merely getting married and having children. Everything God gave us, He gave us in a raw form, but it will take PERSONAL DISCOVERY to reproduce it to suit God's original intent. Out of darkness comes light. When you discover your passion and natural abilities, you will recover from any form of stagnation and come out of obscurity.

For over two decades, I have had the divine privilege of running a teaching ministry for women and mentoring older and younger women. I have seen many women who were confused, hopeless and sad, experience a turnaround after a PERSONAL DISCOVERY of who they were created to be. I totally agree with the wisdom, step-by-step practical and great insights that the author shares in this book.

**Ruth Essien- Founding Pastor, The Flourishing Family Int'l Bible Church & President, Women After Revival Ministry, Lagos Nigeria.**

**An Endorsement for *Personal Discovery for Women***

Hello, women with great minds from all over the world!

Are you going through a tough time in your marriage, career, or ministry? **YOU MUST READ THIS BOOK!**

As many that are in valley of life where confusion is the order of the day, the step-by-step process of how to come out of that valley, are in this book. It will be a blessing to you, as it has also blessed me.

**Pastor Monisola Ajayi, wife of Special Assistant to Continental Overseer/ Country Coordinator of Redeemed Christian Church of God, Turkey.**

I strongly believe this book will transform the lives of many women across the globe, especially those burning with the strong desire to discover and fulfil their purpose. One of the greatest gifts you can give yourself is to discover the real 'you,' and the author, Omokorede, who possesses both professional and life experiences, certainly takes you on that journey. It's indeed worth a read!

**Ojuola Stephen (Founder / CEO), Ladies of Virtue Outreach CIC, & LOVO Women's Day Centre, Southwark, UK.**


Finding your WHY is the most powerful pursuit in the journey of life. This book is therefore a must read for women who want to find their WHY. Women who want to unleash their passion and natural abilities which makes them unique, and Women who are ready to remove every limiting disenfranchising belief in order to embrace the step-by-step approach to discovering who they are and answer the question WHY?"

**Mrs. Modupe Oyekunle, co- Pastor, His Masterpiece Church & National Coordinator Association of Nigerian Women Business Network (ANWBN)**


Attending the "Personal Discovery" workshop organized by Omokorede Fasoro was the practical "light bulb moment " for me. Not only do I understand myself better. I am also better equipped to support other people especially women in their journey.

Life and living is definitely beautiful depending on where you decide to view from. This book is a simple yet definite tool that will bring hope, direction, and inspiration irrespective of where you are as a woman in your life's journey.

**Tinuola Dapo-Awosika, co-Pastor, RCCG, Higher Ground Parish, Lagos Nigeria**

# ACKNOWLEDGEMENTS

And finally, *Personal Discovery for Women* has become a reality!!! Glory to God!!!

First, I would like to appreciate the Almighty God and the Father of Our Lord and Savior Jesus Christ, who has made this dream a reality, after over three years of working on this project. There were several times when I abandoned the task, but the burden to continue and finish up became stronger and stronger day after day.

I appreciate my dear husband and pastor, Ayotunde, for always being there for me, as an encourager and a cheerleader, especially during the wilderness season of my life and while I was working on this book. What could I have done without the support of my beautiful children who have always given me the reason to keep going on? I am grateful to God for the wonderful way you all have turned out. To Him alone be all the glory.

The testimonies shared in this book will not be complete without acknowledging the impact of the life story of my dear mother- Pastor Mrs. Aralola Faturoti - on my life. Thank you for holding forth in the place of prayers and perseverance against all odds. And of course, my younger sister and prayer partner, Ojuola Stephen, for always standing in faith with me on the altar of prayer.

I am also indebted to several men and women of God whose books and messages have over the years been a blessing to me.

A big thank you to all my dear friends (whose names are listed in the endorsement page), who agreed to endorse this book at very short notice. God bless you all.

To all the women that I have had the privilege of being a part of their lives in their quest for purpose. I celebrate and appreciate you all.

Finally, I recognize the effort of Ifeanyi Omeni, for her professional touch in editing this book, and my lovely daughter Oluwabunmi Fasoro for the excellent job done with the beautiful illustrations for this book. Last but not the least, I appreciate the great team at Westbow Press, for the brilliant job they have done in translating this project into reality. Thank you all and God bless you real good.

Thank you all and God bless you real good.

# WHY I WROTE THIS BOOK

For over a decade, I have had the privilege of working with women through the various seminars I conduct, both in corporate and religious gatherings. In my dealings with various categories of women -the very educated and the not-too-educated, the beautiful and the not-so-beautiful, the rich and the poor, I have come to realize that all women have the same basic desires. These desires are the need to be relevant, to make an impact and to find purpose in life. The truth is, many women are confused, disillusioned, discouraged, and frustrated. Many want something deeper than the seemingly satisfying things of a husband and children.

Many have come to realize that there is more to life than merely getting married and having children. I have seen that many women are silently weeping behind the cover of heavy make-up, big head ties, hats and large sunglasses. Many are hurting deep within. Why? They feel that there should be more to their lives than what they have at present.

You see dear friend, I was in such a condition at a time in my life. I had graduated from the university with a particularly good class of degree and was top of my class. I went on to sit for my professional examinations, passed and became a fully registered Quantity Surveyor. I worked for some years in the construction industry and then set up my professional firm. I had a wonderful husband and was blessed with beautiful children. I also had a personal and beautiful relationship with my Maker.

However, deep within me, I knew that something was missing in my life. There was this emptiness, this void within me. I had this sense of purposelessness and frustration with my life. I had also made several unsuccessful attempts at various business ventures which just added to my frustration. I realized that something was missing which I needed to discover. It was later that I was able to realize that **the missing ingredient** was the quest for **PERSONAL DISCOVERY ...** the need to discover who exactly I am.

Dear friend, the truth is ... Until you know who you are as a person, life will have no meaning. Until you discover who you truly are, you will be full of envy, timidity, fear and sometimes bitterness. I recollect that whenever I was in the midst of women who seemed to have it all, and were excelling in their various fields, I would hope and pray that no one should ask me to introduce myself. I simply would not know what to say! It was really that bad!

However, as I embarked on the journey of self-discovery over a period of about ten years, I began to read, research, pray, listen to messages, and attend seminars. During this period which I choose to call the wilderness season of my life, God showed up! He opened my eyes to help me discover who I really am as a person. I discovered that I am a unique being, specially created by God to fulfill a unique purpose. Glory to God!

What then happened? My self-esteem, sense of self-worth, self-value and dignity were restored. I began to see myself the way God saw me, and not the way people saw me, or how circumstances around me defined me. I suddenly discovered a reason for living and to keep going on.

I later realized that my experiences were not unique to me, and that many women like me were going through the same experiences I had gone through during the wilderness season of my life. Some were weeping and groaning, some had even given up all hope; some were even at the point of committing suicide! It is because of this category of women that I was inspired to write this book.

In this book, I will share some of the things I have personally learnt these past couple of years from the Word of God, other books, seminars I attended, and also through researching the lives of others (especially women).

I pray for you, dear friend, that by the time you finish reading this book, every form of confusion and doubt about who you are as a person will be completely gone, in the mighty name of Jesus. Amen.

# WELCOME TO A SEASON OF DISCOVERY!!!

# PART ONE
# Woman, Who are You?

*When you look in the mirror each morning*
*What do you see?*

# CHAPTER ONE

# The Most Important Question of All

*One of the most courageous things you can do is identify
yourself, know who you are, what you believe in and
where you want to go.*

—Sheila Murray Bethel

If someone you had never met before walked up to you and asked
you this three-word question, "Who are you?" what would your
response be?

Assuming the person tells you that you only have one minute to
answer the question, what would your reply be?

A woman? A sister? A wife? A mother?

These are some of the obvious responses most women will give,
are they not?

Dear friend, this is one question that we all will be asked at
one point in our lives. This is one important question that we all
should be able to answer. Imagine getting to the end of your life
only to discover that you had lived the life, hopes, and aspirations
of someone else. What if you found out that you had spent decades

1

of your life pursuing the dreams of another person? The thought of this is quite scary and should get everyone thinking.

Many years ago, a group of deeply religious, very learned, and extremely influential men approached a young man who was making a great impact in society and challenged him. They noticed he was gaining a large followership, even though he was using an unconventional style to get his message across. They approached the young man called John and asked him this same three-word question: Who are you?

> ***Now this is the testimony of John, when the Jews sent priests and Levites from Jerusalem to ask him, "Who are you?"***
>
> **(John 1:19)**

They had seen and heard him preaching powerfully, the message of confession and repentance, and they probably concluded that he must be the Messiah they had been waiting for. When asked this three-word question, he had no hesitation in responding. He was quick to answer them by telling them who he was not. He said to them: "I am not the Christ" **(John1:20)**.

They then began to give him different options (which was probably their way of helping him answer the question, or so they thought). They asked him, "Are you Elijah? Are you the Prophet?"

However, John boldly rejected every label he was offered and every name he was given because he knew for sure who he was.

The truth is this: If you are unable to sincerely answer this question, people will call you what you are not. They will give you labels that they believe suit you, but which God has not given you and what He has not called you.

As they continued to prod John further, he then gave them the summary of who he knew he was as a person, and what he believed God had sent him to do on earth. He said to them:

*I am the voice of one crying in the wilderness;*
*make straight the way of the Lord.*

*(John 1:23)*

John knew for sure that he was neither the Messiah nor the Savior. However, he knew that he had been divinely assigned by God to be the voice and forerunner to prepare the way of the Savior. He lived his life in the fulfillment of this divine assignment till he took his very last breath!

If I were to ask you this same question, what would your response be? Would it be based on who your husband is? The number of children you have? Where you come from? What you do for a living? Or perhaps based on what others have called you?

Let me add another dimension to this question and ask: If you were given just thirty seconds to describe yourself, what would your answer be? How would you describe yourself to people in such a way that they would find you passionate enough to want to either employ you or do business with you? John the Baptist, when confronted with this question over two thousand years ago, gave a specific answer that encapsulated his purpose, his essence, and his assignment here on earth.

This, dear friend, is God's desire for you. He wants you to have a clear picture of who you are, why you are here, and what your assignment on earth is, because He created you for a purpose.

This is what this book will help you discover.

My prayer for you is that by the time you have gone through the pages of this book, you will have a clearer picture of who you truly are as a person and what your God-given purpose is.

# CHAPTER TWO

# Why You Need To Know Who You Are

*There are two great days in a person's life, the day we are born, and the day we discover why.*

—William Barclay

The book, *The Purpose Driven Life*[1] written by American preacher Pastor Rick Warren, was on the New York Times Bestseller list for one of the longest periods in history. It is said to have sold over thirty million copies as of 2012 and by 2020 has been translated into over eighty-five different languages. [2] One would wonder why this book had such a remarkable success rate. The reason might not be far from the fact that it deals with the greatest burden and desire in the heart of every man and woman. This is the need to truly know who one is, the essence of one's life, and what exactly one is here on Earth for.

I remember as a little girl, I would sit in front of the mirror and ask myself questions about my life. I would ask questions like, Who am I? Where did I come from? Why am I here? The questions continued throughout my life until I began to confront the issues and then started to seek answers. I then began to read far and wide, prayed as much as I could, and became desperate for answers.

I would like to mention at this stage the impact of two important books during my search for purpose: *The Assignment*[3] by Dr. Mike Murdoch and *The Purpose Driven Life* by Pastor Rick Warren. I strongly recommend these two books for you to read.

Why do you need to know who you are? What exactly is the big deal about personal discovery?

Personal discovery is the foundation of a purposeful, fulfilling, and impactful life. When you know who you are, life has more meaning and makes more sense to you. Life becomes exciting and this gives you a reason to keep going on, even in the face of challenges.

A life without purpose will be a miserable and frustrating one. Many have maimed and even killed themselves because of this. Some of them are people who we usually think have attained a level of success in their various fields. One cannot help but wonder what will drive a person to a point of taking his or her life, despite being famous and surrounded by so much wealth!

Understandably, some of these suicide cases might have been caused by certain psychological and mental health issues, but the question still is, "What would drive a person to a point of committing suicide, amid plenty?" Could it be the frustration that comes when one has a longing for something deeper, more satisfying, and more authentic than money and fame? Could it possibly be the desire to discover a reason for living that is truly satisfying, which money and riches cannot buy? On the other hand, could it have been triggered by the failure to discover something greater than all these? The discovery of purpose? This truly calls for a lot of concern.

The truth is that when you discover purpose and understand who you are as a person, the discovery frees your heart of all forms of negative emotions such as envy, bitterness, strife, and pride. These are negative emotional vices that can defile and ultimately destroy a person. Medically, it has also been proven that these negative emotions many times lead to certain terminal diseases, depression, and mental illness.

The discovery of purpose also gives you joy, despite the challenges of life. The truth about life is that there will always be seasons when we will be faced with difficulties and problems. It could be the loss of a job or a loved one, a broken marriage, a delay in marriage, or childbirth. The list is endless.

However, when one truly has a revelation of one's assignment in life, the satisfaction of being in the center of God's will brings peace of mind that is beyond human comprehension, no matter the battles being faced. This must have been what kept Joseph going, despite the challenges he faced as a captive slave and then a prisoner, before he finally became a leader in Egypt. He understood that he was still in the center of God's will for his life.

The revelation of who you are as a person also gives your life, direction, and focus. It frees you of every form of distraction. You know what to focus on in life and where to direct your energy. This ultimately leads to excellence and great success in life.

Most of all, when you know who you are, it ultimately builds your self-image and restores your self-esteem. Many people (women in particular) are roaming the streets with battered, bruised, and shattered self-esteem. Many have lost every iota of self-confidence. They cannot see themselves amounting to anything good in life, probably because of the challenges they have faced over the years.

A participant at one of my empowerment seminars said that she did not believe she deserved to have any good thing happening to her. Why would anyone say that about herself, you may ask? You see, she had taken a particular examination several times and had failed each time, so she simply concluded that she was a dullard and a failure! This unfortunately, is the reality of many people.

However, when you discover who you are, life takes a new direction, and you have a better reason to live.

Let us now begin to unravel this question, but first, let me begin by telling you what you are not ...

# CHAPTER THREE

# You Need To Know What You Are Not

*"When the purpose of a thing is not known, abuse is inevitable."*

**(Dr. Myles Munroe)**

In her book, *The Confident woman,* preacher and teacher, Joyce Meyer, notes that in ancient Greek mythology and literature, women were seen as an evil curse that men must endure. She also refers to one of the oldest documents of European literature, Homer's *Iliad,* where she notes that women were presented as the cause of all strife, suffering and misery.[1]

Many other traditions and cultures have different ideas, myths and beliefs about who a woman is. Some see her as a second-class citizen and an inferior creature of God. Others see her as a necessary evil and one that just must be tolerated. Some men see women as mere sex objects, baby factories and part of their earthly possessions! As a result of what some men (and women) have heard repeatedly, they have developed certain perceptions, beliefs, and views about who a woman is. This will then reflect in the way they relate to women in general, and most especially the women in their lives.

Aside from the erroneous way that society perceives women, the challenges facing women globally also affect the way women see themselves. These challenges include female genital mutilation, physical, sexual, emotional, and verbal abuse of all forms, kidnapping, discrimination at home, the workplace, and even sometimes in the church!

The truth is that the degradation and maltreatment of women is a worldwide problem that needs urgent attention. These challenges can damage the self-esteem of the woman. Many women now look at themselves through the lens of societal norms and dictates, and not the way God Almighty- the Creator of all things, sees them. No matter what the opinions of men and society might be, they do not change the original intention or plan of God for the woman.

Let us now go back to the very beginning of all things, to discover why God created the woman.

> *Now the Lord God said, 'It is not good that the man should be <u>alone</u>, I will <u>make</u> him an help meet for him.*
> **(Genesis 2:18)**

The background to this passage is that God had created the heavens and Earth, the animals, the fish of the sea and the plants of the land (Genesis Chapter 1). He then formed man from the soil and placed him in the Garden of Eden, primarily to dress (beautify) and to keep it (protect) it. However, although God saw all the good and beautiful things He had created, He saw that something was missing. Before then, He had seen all the things that He had created and said:

*This is very good.*

**(Genesis 1:31)**

However, when God took a closer look at the man, Adam, He saw that none of the animals could be a suitable companion for him. He discovered that something was not good, and that "something" was missing from his life. What was not good? It was the loneliness of man, the unsuitability of all the other animals God had created, to fulfill the role of companionship in man's life.

God then decided to do something about it. He would **make** another human being that would fill this role in the life of the man and ultimately in the whole of creation. He then caused the man to go into a deep sleep, took one of his ribs, closed the flesh, and **made** the woman.

> *And the Lord God caused a deep sleep to fall on Adam, and he slept; and He took one of his ribs and closed up the flesh in its place. Then the rib which the Lord God had taken from man, He made into a woman and brought her to the man.*

**(Genesis 2:21)**

When Adam woke up from the deep sleep, and saw the woman, he declared excitedly:

> *This is now bone of my bones and flesh of my flesh; she shall be called woman, because she was taken out of man.*

**(Genesis 2:23)**

The above clearly describes how and why the woman was created. She was created to meet a need and to solve a problem, to bring completion and balance to the life of the man, and ultimately the whole of creation. The woman was created to make something that was not good to become good, and even better. Can you imagine what the whole world will be like, without women? It will be one big, bland and boring place! There is a way the presence of a woman adds color, life and vigor to a place.

Likewise, dear friend, you were created to meet a need and to fulfill a purpose. Your life is such that you were created by God to bring sweetness and goodness into the world. Never you doubt that!

It is also interesting to note that the Bible says the woman was **made,** while the man was **formed.** I believe there is a deliberate reason why the Bible uses two different words to describe the process of creation of each of the sexes.

In her book, *Woman, Wife, Mother,* Christian author, Pat Harrison notes that the word formed means to be squeezed together. It is like when a potter is working with a piece of clay to make a pot. On the other hand, she notes that to **make** means to be skillfully and carefully hand-crafted. Is it any wonder therefore, why the woman is so beautifully packaged and well put together by God? She has been carefully hand-crafted by God in a unique and special way! [2]

Dear beautiful daughter of God, your present condition or situation, does not change the fact that you were specially put together by God Almighty Himself. It has been said that every woman, no matter her state, has the potential to look beautiful. Just give her the right condition and resources!

The first woman was created from the most delicate part of the man –his rib cage, which houses the heart. The heart of a man is the real man, the central processing unit of a man (like in a computer). This means that a woman is to be protected, nurtured, nursed, and cared for. She is a rare, treasured, and special commodity before God. He took time to put her together, so that by the time He finished and presented her to the man, he exclaimed, "WOW!"

Furthermore, the woman was created to produce, to carry and

to preserve life. Adam said to her … "She shall be called **woman"** (which simply means a man that has a womb).

This means that God deliberately created the woman with a womb – a place where lives are planted, preserved, and brought forth. This is one major reason why God frowns at abortion. A woman must understand that she is a preserver of live and must do everything possible to do this. Destinies are conceived, preserved, and incubated in the womb.

When Angel Gabriel appeared to Mary, the mother of Jesus, he told her:

> *And behold you shall conceive in your womb and*
> *bring forth a son and shall call his name JESUS.*
> **(Luke 1:31)**

Even before Mary became pregnant, she had been told about the special assignment God had for her womb –to conceive and bring forth a child with a great destiny, who will be the Savior of the world!

Dear friend, if no one has ever told you before now, let me assure you that you have been specially created by God to give and preserve life. Always bear in mind, that every child that passed through (or that will pass through) your womb, is a great destiny waiting to be unfolded, no matter the circumstances of his or her conception.

One highly thought provoking quote that is usually attributed to late Christian author and leader Dr. Myles Munroe[3] is, "…*When the purpose of a thing is not known, abuse is inevitable.*"This is absolutely true. For instance, when you do not understand or know why a certain instrument or appliance has been created, you will misuse it. For instance, if I did not know what a microphone was, and someone placed it in my hands, I could consider using it to beat drums, or to break open a coconut! My ignorance of its purpose will make me unsure of what to use it for.

Therefore, dear friend, you need to understand that you have been skillfully crafted and created by God to meet a need, to solve a problem, to give and to preserve life. Most importantly, you have been created to fulfill a specific and unique purpose and assignment here on Earth, to the glory of God.

David, a shepherd boy who later became a great king of Israel, states this fact in Psalm139:2…

*I will praise you because I have been*
*fearfully and wonderfully made.*

He must have looked at his life, considering the kind of challenging childhood he had had. He was not particularly his father's favorite son. He must have seen how far God had brought him, despite all the challenges he faced in life, and must have concluded that through it all, God had a hand in changing his destiny.

Likewise, beautiful lady, you are not an accident or a mistake, neither are you a genetic error! You are fearfully and wonderfully made!

**YOU BETTER BELIEVE THAT!!**

# CHAPTER FOUR

# Understanding Your Unique Make-Up As A Woman

*Then the rib which the LORD God had taken from man He made into a woman ...*

**(Genesis 1:22)**

I recall a discussion I had with my physician – a gynecologist – a couple of years ago. He explained to me how complicated the physiological make-up (especially the reproductive parts) of a woman is, compared to that of the man. It is certain that God did not make a mistake in creating a woman complete with fallopian tubes, ovaries, uterus, cervix and so on. They are all part of what makes her unique and different so that she can fulfil her God-given roles as a NURTURER, REPRODUCER, MULTIPLIER and PRESERVER OF LIFE.

A woman has been packaged and *wired* by God to be quite different from a man. She is not only different from him physiologically, but also emotionally, psychologically, and physically.

Various scientific studies have proven that men and women think differently, based on the makeup of the human brain. The human brain is said to be mainly made up of two parts- the grey matter (left side of the brain) and the white matter (the right side of the brain). It has been said that women possess more of the white matter, than men. The grey matter is said to be the information processing center of the brain, which deals more with mathematical and logical thinking and can only process one thing at a time. This probably explains why men tend to be very logical in the way they reason and process information.

Women on the other hand, are said to do more of their thinking on the right side (white matter). The white matter is said to network the information processing centers, just like the internet links different computers together across the globe. In this part of the brain, it is believed that more of language and relationship-related thinking takes place. Another interesting fact about this part of the brain is that it has the capacity to multitask at any given time. This probably explains why most women are more expressive verbally and why they are excellent at multitasking.

In her book, *The Power of Women,* Susan Nolen- Hoeksema stated that women have mental identity, emotional and relational strengths which can be effectively harnessed and utilized by them to lead others around them to better lives. A woman has great abilities and potentials to positively affect her generation.[1]

Isn't that amazing? The sad truth, however, is that most women lack this understanding, but rather have an awfully bad impression about themselves! I would like to end this chapter with a poem I wrote a couple of years ago, which I believe truly summarizes the essence and strength of a woman ...

## WHO AM I?

I am ...

- *A female human being*
- *A "man" with a womb*
- *God's handiwork*
- *God's masterpiece*
- *God's workmanship*
- *Created for a specific purpose*
- *Created to meet a need.*
- *Created to solve a problem*
- *Beautiful to behold.*
- *Custodian of life*
- *Preserver of life*
- *One who brought completion*
- *To God's work of creation*
- *Nothing was good,*
- *Until I, the woman showed up.*
- *Even God confirmed this!*

*I am a woman, and I am proud to be one.*

# CHAPTER FIVE

# Understanding Your Unique Make-Up As A Person

*"You were born an original, don't die a copy."*
**(John Mason)**

Aside from the fact that women are unique and quite different from men, it is also necessary to note that even as individuals, we have been specially packaged by God, to fulfill unique purposes, irrespective of our sexes.

Have you ever wondered why embassies are always quick to collect fingerprints of visa applicants who want to come to their countries? It has been proven that no two fingerprints are alike. Not even those of identical twins. Each person has a unique set of fingerprints that can never be matched with another person's. Aside from the uniqueness of our fingerprints, it is also interesting to note that each person is made up of millions of cells which contain his or her unique DNA (Deoxyribonucleic acid) and genes. These genes (which are a combination of what each of us has received from our parents), are what determine our unique features. In essence, no one has the exact combination of your genes and DNA! You are an original! How awesome and amazing this is!

While growing up as a young girl in the eighties, I suffered from a form of identity crisis. I hated who I was and what I looked like. Why? I was a skinny teenage girl, who was almost 6 feet tall! Most times, I was the tallest person in my class and sometimes, in the entire school! I was bullied because of my height and called derogatory names such as skinny, *tallie* etc. There were times I hated to walk on the streets of the neighborhood where my family lived at that time. I could be walking on the street, and someone would call me derogatory names, while driving past. I almost became a recluse and an anti-social being. I found escape and joy in my schoolbooks and novels. All these negative names had a serious effect on my self-esteem and self-confidence. However, I came across a particular passage of scripture many years after, which liberated me …

> ***Before I formed you in your mother's womb, I knew you and ordained you a prophet unto the nations.***
>
> **(Jeremiah 1:5)**

In the passage above, God spoke to a young man called Jeremiah, who was possibly battling with a form of low self-esteem. This was at a time when his people (the Israelites) had become captives in a strange land. He had probably concluded that he was useless and a good-for-nothing, when he considered the hopelessness of his state and nation. However, during this chaos, God spoke to him and gave him words of encouragement as found in the book of Jeremiah 1:5.

God assured Jeremiah that He knew about him, even before he was conceived in his mother's womb. In essence, he existed as an idea in God's mind, before his parents came together. God went on to add that He not only knew about him, but had ordained (appointed, commissioned, and anointed) him as a prophet to the nations. A prophet is simply someone who is God's mouthpiece; someone who speaks God's will and counsel in various aspects of life. As long as you are a child of God, know that He also wants you to be His mouthpiece in your area of influence. Therefore, it is important to discover your area of influence.

The world we are in desperately needs people who will speak the counsel and will of God in the media, in government, in politics, in science, in education and so on. Imagine what kind of world we would have if we had the likes of Daniel, Joseph and Esther running our nations? How awesome this will be!

Back to the story of Jeremiah. God's message to him, from Jeremiah 1:5 must have been a very encouraging and uplifting message for him. The impact of all God said to him in that chapter, ushered him into an assignment that spanned many more years.

Do you know that this same truth also applies to you and me? God thought about you even before you were born on earth. As a matter of fact, you did not come into existence just because your parents had sex with each other. You came into being because God had already envisioned the **idea** and **wonder** called you, in His mind. He had conceived what you would look like, your sex, your tastes, your strengths, your likes and dislikes, your skin color and so on. Most of all, He had decided on the purpose for which He created you, and the assignment which He was sending you to Planet Earth to accomplish for Him. God also decided the best family, town and nation for you to be born into, that will help you fulfill your God-given assignment here on earth.

It was after God had finished putting together the beautiful idea called you that your parents came together, so that your conception could take place.

How awesome!

This is true, whether your parents planned to give birth to you. Even if you are a child of an unwed woman or a product of rape, it does not change the fact that you were on God's mind. I once heard someone use this phrase *"...There are no illegitimate children, only illegitimate parents."* In other words, whatever the channel through which you came into this world; no matter how unpleasant it was, whether your parents were married or not, God conceived your idea, your purpose, your assignment, and your mission here on earth, even before your parents met. How amazing and encouraging this is!

When I received the revelation from this passage, hope and life were restored into my heart. I understood that God took time first to conceive the idea called me, and then He packaged my whole being to suit the specific assignment He has for me here on Earth. I realized that my physical form is perfect. I did not feel like a recluse anymore. I was confident in my own skin and loved who I was and how I had been packaged by God! What a liberating truth that was for me!

I encourage you also, dear sister, that you not only embrace this truth, but that you believe it with all your heart.

Why not say these words out loud now.

*"I was an idea in God's mind, specially envisioned in His mind, even before my mother and father conceived me. My mother and father had to conceive me, so that the wonder called me can be revealed to this world! I am a wonder to my world!!!"*

# CHAPTER SIX

———— ∿ ————

## Specially Packaged To Fulfill
## A Unique Purpose

*"God tailored the curves of your life to fit an empty space in His jigsaw puzzle ... God packed you on purpose for a purpose."*

**(Max Lucado)**

When discussing the subject of **Purpose**, it is impossible to leave out God, who is the Originator, Initiator and Creator of all things. The first thing to do therefore, when you want to discover purpose, is to **Look up**. It entails looking up to God for direction, asking Him, in the place of prayers, to reveal His purpose for our lives and trusting Him to do so. It is obvious that when you want to know, unearth, or discover the purpose of a thing, the best person to ask is the manufacturer of that product, or the manufacturer's manual which describes the product. This is one reason why the subject of purpose begins and ends with God. It is about discovering the original intention in God's mind -Why He created us and for what specific purpose.

In his award-winning book, *The Purpose Driven Life*, Rick Warren notes that:

> *"God never does anything accidentally and He never makes mistakes. He has a reason for everything He creates. Every plant and every animal were planned by God, and every person was designed with a purpose in mind ... God is not haphazard; He planned it all with great precision."* [1]

What then is purpose?

To answer the question, let me begin with what purpose is not.

Your purpose in life is not about what you own. It is not about where you work or what you do. It is also not about your status in society, neither is it about your achievements. Rather, it is about discovering God's original intention or plan for your life and living every day of your life in its pursuit.

Everything God created on Earth has a purpose, and it is certain, as was mentioned in the last chapter, that every one of us was sent by God to fulfill a specific assignment on Earth. Do you know that even the rat that we so very much despise has its place in the eco-system? Environmentalists say that it helps to clean up garbage and waste by eating it up. Scientists say that rats are also excellent for laboratory tests because their metabolic system is identical to humans. If an ordinary rat has a purpose and a reason for its existence, how much more you and me?

To discover purpose is to discover the reason for your existence; to find out what was in God's mind when He put the wonder called you, together and placed you in your mother's womb. In the words of Christian author Max Lucado, purpose is finding out how you fit into *"God's jigsaw puzzle"* [2]

The truth, dear friend, is that a person has not truly started living, until he or she discovers God's purpose for his or her life. When you discover purpose, it produces joy in your heart, a deep sense of fulfillment and peace of mind. Purpose gives you strength to persevere, even in the face of the challenges of life. It gives you energy and passion that motivates you. As you pursue your passion wholeheartedly, it leads to excellence. Excellence ultimately attracts success, wealth, and fame. The pursuit of purpose, therefore, is the secret of true greatness in life.

It is important to also add that God's purpose for your life is something good. It is your contribution to the world, your own part in making the world a better place. Your purpose is a solution to someone's problem, the answer to someone's prayers, and the blessing someone needs.

- When Mother Theresa discovered purpose, the extremely sick and the dying on the streets of Calcutta, got an answer to their prayers.
- When William Wilberforce discovered purpose, it was an answer to the prayers of the men and women who were being forcefully taken from the shores of Africa, to be sold as slaves in other parts of the world.
- When Jonas Salk discovered purpose, it brought joy and peace to the millions of people that could either have died or been maimed with polio, because he came up with the polio vaccine.
- When Martin Luther King Jr. discovered purpose, segregation amongst the whites and blacks in the United States of America, became a thing of the past.

The list is endless.

The Bible is also full of men and women who discovered purpose and changed their world.

People like Joseph who was used by God to deliver the whole

world from a potential global food crisis, because he interpreted Pharaoh's dream and gave him a solution to the forthcoming famine.

> *This will happen just as I have described it, for God has revealed to Pharaoh in advance what he is about to do. The next seven years will be a period of great prosperity throughout the land of Egypt. But afterward there will be seven years of famine so great that all the prosperity will be forgotten in Egypt. Famine will destroy the land. This famine will be so severe that even the memory of the good years will be erased. As for having two similar dreams, it means that these events have been decreed by God, and he will soon make them happen. Therefore, Pharaoh should find an intelligent and wise man and put him in charge of the entire land of Egypt. Then Pharaoh should appoint supervisors over the land and let them collect one-fifth of all the crops during the seven good years. Have them gather all the food produced in the good years that are just ahead and bring it to Pharaoh's storehouses. Store it away, and guard it so there will be food in the cities. That way, there will be enough to eat when the seven years of famine come to the land of Egypt. Otherwise, this famine will destroy the land.*

**(Genesis 41:28-36)**

There was Moses whose purpose, over 400 years after, was to deliver his people from slavery and from the clutches of Pharaoh.

> *Then the LORD told him, "I have certainly seen the oppression of my people in Egypt. I have heard*

*their cries of distress because of their harsh slave drivers. Yes, I am aware of their suffering. So I have come down to rescue them from the power of the Egyptians and lead them out of Egypt into their own fertile and spacious land. It is a land flowing with milk and honey—the land where the Canaanites, Hittites, Amorites, Perizzites, Hivites, and Jebusites now live. Look! The cry of the people of Israel has reached me, and I have seen how harshly the Egyptians abuse them. Now go, for I am sending you to Pharaoh. You must lead my people Israel out of Egypt.*

**(Exodus 3:7-10)**

A young girl called Esther was divinely positioned by God to be in the palace at a time when her people would have been annihilated by the evil Haman.

*Mordecai sent this reply to Esther: "Don't think for a moment that because you're in the palace you will escape when all other Jews are killed. If you keep quiet at a time like this, deliverance and relief for the Jews will arise from some other place, but you and your relatives will die. Who knows if perhaps you were made queen for just such a time as this?*

**(Esther 4:13-14)**

Just as these men and women and many others fulfilled purpose and affected their generations positively, it is time for you to put your name on the list of world changers, as you also discover and fulfill purpose.

In addition to looking up to the Almighty God, the One who

created us all with a purpose in mind, it is also important for us to take a keen look at other aspects of our lives. We should:

- Look behind.
- Look within.
- Look around.
- Look ahead.

It is also necessary to take a step backward, to **Look behind** and consider some experiences you have had in the past, especially if there are patterns that have been established in your life over time. These could be pointers to what God wants you to focus on in life. The second part of this book will focus on this aspect.

Next, is the need to **Look within**. This entails you taking a good look at what God has placed inside you. The truth is that God has uniquely packaged each of us with the right gifts, abilities, resources, and personalities that will help us fulfill this purpose. There is a reason why you can do certain things better than others, and why you have a certain personality type.

I like the way Rick Warren puts it in his book ...

> *"God prescribed every single detail of your body. He deliberately chose your race, the color of your skin, your hair, and every other feature. He custom made your body just the way he wanted it. He also determined the natural talents you would possess and the uniqueness of your personality ... God also planned where you would be born and where you would live for His purpose."* [3]

To **Look around** means to be sensitive enough to pay keen attention to things around you that always seem to get your attention. What do you see that others do not see? What catches your fancy when you enter a store, a house, or a supermarket? This is usually a pointer to things you have a passion for. The second part of this book will also focus on this.

Finally, there is the need for you to **Look ahead.** This entails crafting a vision and painting a picture of your future, based on some dreams you have had, probably from a young age.

It's important for you to realize that you are here on a mission, on an assignment and with a heavenly mandate, to fulfill destiny and purpose.

As a matter of fact, the Bible refers to us in Ephesians 2:10 as God's Masterpiece and His unique work of art.

> *For we are God's masterpiece. He has created us anew in Christ Jesus, so we can do the good things he planned for us long ago.*
> **(Ephesians 2:10 - NLT)**

The Oxford learner's dictionary describes the word, masterpiece, as "a work of art such as a painting, movie, book, etc. that is an excellent, or the best, example of the artist's work"[4] Another online dictionary puts it this way... "a work done with extraordinary skill, *especially*: a supreme intellectual or artistic achievement"[5]

I will simply describe a masterpiece as *"a unique work of art that give you the wow feeling when you see it!"*

As a matter of fact, an artist's or a musician's greatest piece of work is also referred to as his or her masterpiece. Examples of these are:

- The Monalisa painting by Leonardo da Vinci
- The statue of David by Michelangelo
- The Sistine Chapel painting, also by Michelangelo.
- The Messiah musical piece, written by George Frederick Handel, and so many more ...

Likewise, you are a unique work of art. Not only are you unique, but you are also outstanding, special and a wonder to behold. Can you now begin to imagine how exceptional you are to God? You are an exclusive and rare creation of His. You are simply one of a kind!

There is no other person in this world that is just like you, who has the exact combination of qualities that God has placed inside you.

How awesome this is!

In addition to this, you were an idea in God's mind, even before your parents came together to conceive you. You have been specially designed and put together by God to meet a need and to solve a problem. You will do yourself and the world a disservice when you fail to discover your purpose. It is your responsibility to discover this purpose and to fulfill it.

In summary,

- You were born at the right time,
- To the right family,
- In the right place,
- In the right country,
- In the right season,
- With the right qualities
- To fulfill a specific assignment at a time like this.
- You are simply UNIQUE!

What then are the things that make each of us unique? Pastor Rick Warren came up with the concept of **SHAPE,**[6] an acronym for five capabilities that he believes God has placed inside us to help us discover and fulfill purpose. It stands for S- Spiritual gifts, H- Heart, A- Abilities, P-Personality and E- Experiences. Max Lucado refers to this concept as the **SWEET SPOT.**[7] According to him, this sweet spot is an intersection between your strengths (what you do), where you do it and why you do it (for God's glory).

After years of personal study and research in different resources, including the Word of God, and also by divine inspiration, I have come up with a list of five qualities that I believe give a simple and straightforward formula for the pursuit of Personal Discovery. I refer to these qualities as the **FIVE PETALS (5Ps) OF PERSONAL DISCOVERY.**™ I strongly believe that these five petals will help you clarify various aspects of your life, as you look above, within, behind and around you. The second part of this book will reveal more about these petals.

# PART TWO
# Unveiling the Five Petals
# of Personal Discovery™

# CHAPTER SEVEN

# About the Five Petals (5Ps)

*"A rose can never be a sunflower, and a sunflower can never be a rose. All flowers are beautiful in their own way, and that's like women too."*

**(Miranda Kerr)**

Many women would love to receive a bouquet of beautiful flowers from that incredibly special person. However, it is likely that few have taken the time to take a good look at the various parts of flowers and what makes them so beautiful. In this section, I have written about flowers.

Now, you might be wondering, 'What this has this got to do with the subject of purpose and personal discovery?' You will get to know why, soon …

A flower is that special part of a plant which bears the seeds. All flowers have petals which are actually modified leaves. They are the colored parts of flowers and usually come in exceptionally beautiful colors and shapes, depending on the type of plant. They cover the reproductive parts of flowers and make it easy for insects to find flowers so they can be pollinated, by attracting them with their sweet smell. When pollination takes place, the plant produces and disperses its seeds. This sets the stage for reproduction to take place and subsequently, fruitfulness. Why is this so? Because, inside every seed lies its potential to become a tree and, in a tree, lies a potential forest. In the words of Dr. Myles Munroe, *"I hold a forest in my hand ... in every seed there is a tree."*[1] Therefore, petals are an important part of a plant.

Just as every type of flower has its unique kind of petals, we also have qualities that are peculiar to each of us. The truth is that there are no two people that are born with the same combination of qualities. This also applies to identical twins born within minutes or seconds of each other. Even if they look 100% alike, there will still be some remarkable differences in their personalities and the likes.

In the rest of this book, I will refer to these unique set of qualities as the **FIVE PETALS OF PERSONAL DISCOVERY™ (or 5Ps of PD).** I chose to use petals as an example because of what they stand for and what they represent in plants.

Just as the petals of a flower attract insects for its pollination, the moment you begin to unveil and display your own unique petals (qualities) and you start to use them for God's glory, you begin to walk in the center of God's purpose for your life. As you do this, you then attract the favor of God into your life. Purpose brings favor with God and favor with man.

A good example of purpose attracting favor was a young man called Joseph. Despite the challenging situation he found himself in, first as a slave in the household of Potiphar, and later as a prisoner, he found favor, both with God and with his masters as he displayed his "petals."

*The LORD was with Joseph, and he was a successful man; and he was in the house of his master the Egyptian. And his master saw that the LORD was with him and that the LORD made all he did to prosper in his hand. So Joseph found favor in his sight, and served him. Then he made him overseer of his house, and all that he had he put under his authority. So it was, from the time that he had made him overseer of his house and all that he had, that the LORD blessed the Egyptian's house for Joseph's sake; and the blessing of the LORD was on all that he had in the house and in the field. Thus he left all that he had in Joseph's hand, and he did not know what he had except for the bread which he ate.*

(Genesis 39:2-6)

*Then Joseph's master took him and put him into the prison, a place where the king's prisoners were confined. And he was there in the prison. But the LORD was with Joseph and showed him mercy, and He gave him favor in the sight of the keeper of the prison. And the keeper of the prison committed to Joseph's hand all the prisoners who were in the prison; whatever they did there, it was his doing. The keeper of the prison did not look into anything that was under Joseph's authority, because the LORD was with him; and whatever he did, the LORD made it prosper.*

(Genesis 39:20-23)

In the context of what we have been discussing about flowers and petals, I strongly believe that a woman who has unveiled and displayed her "petals" so to speak, will always attract the favor of God, just as the flower does not need to chase or attract insects for pollination. A purpose-driven woman always has a sweet aroma which is appealing at all times.

What then are these Five petals of Personal Discovery™?
They are:

1.  **Physical Appearance-** The way you look, which is unique to you. You are the right height, right shape, and the right size. Do not desire to look like someone else! Appreciate and celebrate the way you look!

2.  **Personality** – This is your emotional make-up, your temperament, the unique way you react to circumstances or situations and the way you relate to people. It is the way you perceive and see things.

3.  **Passion-** These are your hopes, affections, aspirations and what you really love. Everyone is passionate about something. For some, it is looking after children, the sick or the elderly; for some it is cars, books, animals and so on. There is a reason why God gives someone a passion for one thing, and another, a passion for something else.

4.  **Potentials-**These are your natural abilities, gifts, and talents. They are inherent in you from birth and need to be developed and used for God's glory. The truth is that everybody has at least one talent. It could be the ability to sing, to write, to dance, to draw … the list is endless.

5.  **Past Experiences-**These are circumstances that have come your way in life, some of which were beyond your control, which have molded you. Sometimes, God allows us to go through some challenges, because of the assignment He has for us, or some problems He has created for us to solve.

We shall look at each of these qualities in more details in subsequent chapters.

# CHAPTER EIGHT

# Your Physical Appearance Is Unique To You

*I will praise you because I am fearfully and wonderfully made. Marvelous are your works, and that my soul knows very well.*

**(Psalm 139 -14)**

Many times, as women, we get carried away by the quest to make ourselves look more beautiful. Some women go the extra mile at the expense of many other important things so that they can look more attractive than the woman next door.

A short woman wishes she were taller; a fat one, that she were slimmer, a dark-skinned woman wants to be lighter, while a light-skinned one wants to go for a suntan! It is amazing how women go all out to outdo themselves! Some women are simply not satisfied with the way they look and so they keep looking for other people to validate them. This is very unhealthy, as it is the root cause of a low self-esteem.

However, the moment a woman realizes that God has uniquely packaged her with the right physical structure and appearance to help her fulfill her purpose, she is encouraged and strengthened from within.

Do you know for instance that the color of your skin was predetermined by God? It surely did not take Him by surprise. He gave you the right skin color to help you fulfill your destiny. Can I also add that your height, no matter how short or tall you are, has been given to you by God to help you fulfill purpose. The likes of Magic Johnson and Shaquille O'Neal are extremely tall men whose heights help them excel as basketball stars.

Have you ever wondered why some women appear to have masculine features? Could it be that God has uniquely packaged them that way because He has an assignment for them in sports? Take a look at some of them and you will begin to have a feel of what I am talking about. A particular Nigerian female sprinter who ruled the world of female athletics in the 1980s, comes to mind. It was clear that her male-like physique added to her strength and stamina as a sprinter. It is disturbing that in these present days, such women would have been told that they have the wrong body and encouraged to have a sex change. However, God never makes a mistake.

Do you also know that what you seem to lack in your physical make-up and appearance cannot limit the fulfillment of God's purpose for your life? Helen Keller became blind, deaf, and dumb at eighteen months after an illness. She could have lived her life in frustration and as a nonentity. However, with the help of a dedicated teacher called Anne Sullivan (whom her parents hired to look after her), she eventually learnt to read and write. She went on to attend university, learnt to speak in three different languages, wrote her autobiography and even directed a film about her life! Before she died, she became a greatly sought-after speaker and her story has continued to challenge many people across nations of the world, many years after her death.

A few years ago, I came across the video of a young man called Nick Vujicic.[1] As I sat before the TV screen watching him in amazement, I began to wonder how a person like him could ever be happy in life. I watched him brushing his hair and his teeth, taking a dive in the swimming pool, and even riding a horse! He seemed to be on top of the world and in high spirits! I also saw him preaching the gospel to a congregation of hundreds of people, as he encouraged them to have hope and not lose heart. You see, the amazing thing about Nick is that he was born without hands and legs. All he has is a tiny toe underneath his torso which he uses to type and operate his electric wheelchair![2]

The story of Nick is an amazing one that should motivate and encourage anyone who listens to it. He was born in 1982 to the family of Pastor and Mrs. Boris Vujicic. Without any prior warning about what was to come, he arrived as their first-born son in 1982, born without arms and legs. Nick grew up having to deal with various issues of low self-esteem, bullying, depression and wondering why God chose to create him that way.

However, he had an encounter with The Lord Jesus Christ and surrendered his life to Him. He then discovered from the Word of God that irrespective of his serious physical abnormalities, God still has a unique purpose for his life.

Now, Nick goes all over the world sharing his testimony, inspiring and motivating others to turn to Christ. A couple of years ago, he got married to a beautiful lady and they are now blessed with four lovely children, including a set of twins! Only God could have given him such a beautiful life.

You see dear friend, no matter how physically, mentally, economically and socially challenged you might be, God is still more than able to use all these to fulfill His purpose through you, and in you.

Dear friend, never you despise your physical appearance. Just ensure that you are always well dressed and present yourself in a nice way that will enhance your looks. There are lots of magazines and books out there with information on the right styles that fit various body shapes.

Embrace who you are and what you have and begin to thank God, because your physical make-up is unique to you.

**Why not make this declaration now?**

*I (put your name) am fearfully and wonderfully made by God.*

*I declare that I have a great destiny and a unique purpose in life.*

*I have the right height, shape, size, looks and so on, to help me fulfill my destiny.*

*I have been born for a time like this into the right family, in the right town and the right nation.*

*I am a wonder about to unfold and emerge, to the glory of God! So, help me, God.*

# CHAPTER NINE

# Your Personality Is The Real You

*For You formed my inward parts: You covered me in my mother's womb.*

**(Psalm 139:13)**

In her book titled *Personality Plus*[1] Florence Littauer describes Personality as "*...temperament, the real you ... the dress you put on.*"

The Cambridge online dictionary describes it as "*the special combination of qualities in a person that makes that person different from others, as shown by the way the person behaves, feels, and thinks....*"[2]

I like to describe it as "your emotional make-up." Your temperament or personality type explains why you think the way you do, why you reason or respond the way you do, under different circumstances and situations. It explains why you are different from the other person, in your tastes, likes, and dislikes.

Let me add here, that your personality does not relate to any wrong or sinful habit you might be harboring in your life. It would therefore be out of place, to say for instance that, "*Lying is my personality or outbursts of anger are a display of my personality traits!*"

Your personality captures your emotional strengths and weaknesses as a person. It is what God has placed in you to contribute to others and to the community at large. It is the totality of your psychological, intellectual, emotional, and physical characteristics. It is the expression of yourself and the perception of others about you.

When you truly discover your personality type, it will put you on the path to self-discovery. The understanding of your personality will help you discover the career path or business that suits you best. It will also help you to know the contributions you are designed to bring to the world and to any group you belong to. Your personality also affects how and where you use your gifts and abilities. The truth is that you can only be your best at being yourself. It will be unfair to call a fish a failure, just because it is unable to climb a tree, or to conclude that a monkey is a failure just because it cannot swim!

There is no good or bad personality type. Each one has its major strengths and weaknesses, what motivates it and how it responds emotionally. Also, when making decisions or when under pressure, each personality type responds in different ways. Each personality type has its unique combination of traits. It is however possible to combine some traits from two different personality types, although one will be more dominant than the other. The truth is, dear friend, it is your responsibility as a person to discover and understand your personality, so that you can know how to manage it effectively. This is also the foundation of emotional intelligence – being self-aware.

Psychologists worldwide have done a lot of work on this subject. Although there are many schools of thought on the fact that there are different variations of the personality types. However, they all built on the foundation of the four basic types namely, **Sanguine, Choleric, Melancholic**, and **Phlegmatic**. Some also refer to them as Dominant, Influencing, Steady and Conscientious (DISC) personality types. I have also had the privilege at the home front, of learning first-hand about these different personality types, by observing and parenting my uniquely different children, over the last twenty plus years. It has been a genuinely interesting experience.

I like to refer to the major personality types using four simple phrases that I came up with …

For the Dominant (Choleric), I like to refer to them as **The Bold ones**, the Influencing personalities (Sanguine) as **The Bubbly ones.** I refer to those with The Steady personality (Phlegmatic) as **The Blissful ones** and the Conscientious (Melancholic), as **The Balanced ones.**

1. **THE BOLD ONES** – are people with dominant personalities and qualities. They like to be in control of others, are overly aggressive and always want to lead and take charge, rather than follow. They always enjoy a cooperative and challenging environment. These bold ones, also called Directors are adventurous, bold, firm, persistent and daring and are always ready to take on any risk. They tend to be independent, resourceful, and very productive. I have a son who is unmistakably a dominant personality and is quick to give directions and instructions to everyone at home, including me his mother! I have had to remind him several times who the parent is, at home!

As was mentioned before, every personality type has its strengths and weaknesses. The major weakness of the Directors is the fact that they are not very patient people. They tend to be intolerant with people, as they feel they are slowing them down. They can also be overbearing, blunt and too demanding. People that fall into this category need to constantly pray for patience and gentleness.

These set of people will however do very well in careers, professions or ministries that are daring, tasking and will give them opportunities to take up leadership positions where they can lead others, such as Law, Politics, the Armed forces, and the likes.

Paul the Apostle was clearly someone with a dominant personality. He was bold, daring, vocal and fearless and was even ready to go to places that others believed were too dangerous for him.

On one occasion, he had a clash with Apostle Peter, and was quick to reprimand him …

> *Now when Peter had come to Antioch, I withstood him to his face, because he was to be blamed; for before certain men came from James, he would eat with the Gentiles; but when they came, he withdrew and separated himself, fearing those who were of the circumcision. And the rest of the Jews also played the hypocrite with him, so that even Barnabas was carried away with their hypocrisy.*
>
> *(Galatians 2:11)*

At another time, he had been warned about the dangers that lay ahead of him if he made a particular trip. What was his response?

> *And as we stayed many days, a certain prophet named Agabus came down from Judea. When he had come to us, he took Paul's belt, bound his own hands and feet, and said, "Thus says the Holy Spirit, 'So shall the Jews at Jerusalem bind the man who owns this belt, and deliver him into the hands of the Gentiles.' "Now when we heard these things, both we and those from that place pleaded with him not to go up to Jerusalem. Then Paul answered, "What do you mean by weeping and breaking my heart? For I am ready not only to be bound, but also to die at Jerusalem for the name of the Lord Jesus." So when he would not be persuaded, we ceased, saying, "The will of the Lord be done."*
>
> *(Acts 21: 10-14)*

Bold and daring!

It was obvious that it was God who *wired* Apostle Paul with this fearless trait right from birth. He displayed this when he was an enemy of the Church, going from house to house arresting and persecuting Christians (Acts 8:3). After his conversion, he went on to use this same strong and dominant personality to accomplish great things for the sake of the gospel.

Are you a dominant personality? Are you bold, fearless, and daring? Have people told you to slow down, just because according to them, a woman should only be seen and not heard? In such instances, it will be great to tell such people about women in the Bible like Deborah – a bold and daring woman who graciously combined her roles as a wife, a mother a prophetess and a judge in the land …

> *Now Deborah, a prophetess, the wife of Lapidoth, was judging Israel at that time. And she would sit under the palm tree of Deborah between Ramah and Bethel in the mountains of Ephraim. And the children of Israel came up to her for judgment. Then she sent and called for Barak the son of Abinoam from Kedesh in Naphtali, and said to him, "Has not the LORD God of Israel commanded, 'Go and deploy troops at Mount Tabor; take with you ten thousand men of the sons of Naphtali and of the sons of Zebulun; and against you. I will deploy Sisera, the commander of Jabin's army, with his chariots and his multitude at the River Kishon; and I will deliver him into your hand'?" And Barak said to her, "If you will go with me, then I will go; but if you will not go with me, I will not go!"*
>
> *So she said, "I will surely go with you; nevertheless there will be no glory for you in the journey you*

*are taking, for the LORD will sell Sisera into the hand of a woman." Then Deborah arose and went with Barak to Kedesh. And Barak called Zebulun and Naphtali to Kedesh; he went up with ten thousand men under his command, and Deborah went up with him. Then Deborah said to Barak, "Up! For this is the day in which the LORD has delivered Sisera into your hand. Has not the LORD gone out before you?" So Barak went down from Mount Tabor with ten thousand men following him. And the LORD routed Sisera and all his chariots and all his army with the edge of the sword before Barak; and Sisera alighted from his chariot and fled away on foot. But Barak pursued the chariots and the army as far as Harosheth Hagoyim, and all the army of Sisera fell by the edge of the sword; not a man was left.*

(Judges 4:4-10, 14-16)

2. **THE BUBBLY ONES** – As the name implies, these are people with a very lively personality. They are great influencers, energetic, enthusiastic, very social, and cheerful. They are also referred to as cheerleaders and are always optimistic and tend to see the bright side of everything. They are usually bright and colourful, and they love working with people and groups. They like to inspire and charm others and always enjoy popularity. They are usually the life of the party or of any gathering of people.

I used to have an issue with one of my daughters who incidentally falls into this category. I felt she was too active and jumpy, and I used to see her as being kind of light-hearted. However, the moment she graduated from elementary school and left home for boarding school (high school), the house became extremely dull. It then occurred to me that she was, as a matter of fact, the life of the house! She always used to make things happen at the home front and created so much fun activities for everyone in the family. The rest of us seemed to be a boring bunch!

Their weakness, however, is that they have the tendency to be disorganised, impulsive, and forgetful! They are also too trusting, and many times people tend to take advantage of them. I guess this should be obvious, considering the kind of people they are.

Such people need to pray for grace to be more organized and focused. These amazing set of people will do well in careers or businesses that regularly connect them with people, such as Customer Service, Media, Acting, Events Planning and the likes.

Apostle Peter was clearly a cheerleader who also had a lively personality. He was always ready to jump into conclusions and say things, even without really taking time to think them through. For instance, when the Lord Jesus Christ announced his death, Peter was quick to respond. At another time, when He saw Jesus walking on water, he was hasty to join Him, but then began to sink shortly after …

> *But immediately Jesus spoke to them, saying, "Be of good cheer! It is I; do not be afraid." And Peter answered Him and said, "Lord, if it is You, command me to come to You on the water." So He said, "Come." And when Peter had come down out of the boat, he walked on the water to go to Jesus. But when he saw that the wind was boisterous, he was afraid; and beginning to sink, he cried out, saying, "Lord, save me!*
>
> *(Matthew 14:27-30)*

Later, when a group of people came to arrest Jesus in the Garden of Gethsemane, yet again, he was quick to react.

Bubbly and lively!

*And Judas, who betrayed Him, also knew the place; for Jesus often met there with His disciples. Then Judas, having received a detachment of troops, and officers from the chief priests and Pharisees, came there with lanterns, torches, and weapons. Jesus therefore, knowing all things that would come upon Him, went forward and said to them, "Whom are you seeking?" They answered Him, "Jesus of Nazareth." Jesus said to them, "I am He." And Judas, who betrayed Him, also stood with them. Now when He said to them, "I am He," they drew back and fell to the ground. Then He asked them again, "Whom are you seeking?" And they said, "Jesus of Nazareth." Jesus answered, "I have told you that I am He. Therefore, if you seek Me, let these go their way," that the saying might be fulfilled which He spoke," Of those whom You gave Me I have lost none."*

*Then Simon Peter, having a sword, drew it and struck the high priest's servant, and cut off his right ear. The servant's name was Malchus.*

*So Jesus said to Peter, "Put your sword into the sheath. Shall I not drink the cup which My Father has given Me?*

*(John18:2-11)*

Despite his jumpy and hyperactive nature, Apostle Peter went on to become a mighty tool in God's hands. Are you a bubbly personality? Celebrate who you are! The world needs people like you. God needs people like you and wants to make you a mighty vessel in His hands.

3. **THE BLISSFUL ONES** People that fall into this group are usually very easygoing, accommodating and tend to get along with most people around them. They are noticeably quiet, calm, reserved, warm, tolerant, and usually contended with any situation they find themselves. They are also referred to as caregivers, because they are always looking out for the good of others. In a group of people or in a family, there is one person who tends to always be the peace maker and the mother hen in the group or family. That person is the caregiver.

Interestingly, my husband and I are also blessed with a daughter who fits this description perfectly, and this has helped me understand the make-up of this remarkably interesting set of people. She is the type that could sit in one spot all day long without being bothered or bothering anyone about anything. She would always try as much as possible not to get into anyone's way. At a time when my children were much younger, I would compare her with her livelier older sister and conclude that she (the older one) needed to be cautioned to slow down and be gentle like her "caregiver" sister. However, as I matured as a parent and had a clearer understanding of personality types, I realized that each child is unique and should be allowed to express himself or herself, with proper parental guidance.

What I also found amusing was that when it was time to discipline either of them, what worked for one would not work for the other! The lively one hated being confined to a corner as a form of punishment. However, this was always a delight for the caregiver one who hated being asked to do anything physical or one that involved any form of action. Funny, isn't it? These examples just show how different we are, and how we respond to various situations, based on our personality types.

If you feel that this describes the kind of person you are, some jobs to consider for yourself could be Counseling, Medicine, Nursing, and the likes.

Blissful and calm!

In as much as the caregivers sound wonderful, they also display some traits that need to be worked on, such as the fact that they tend to be complacent, laid back and resistant to change. They hate confrontation and will rather suffer in silence than address burning issues.

Father Abraham was like this. When there were problems between his workers and those of his younger nephew, Lot, he avoided confrontation and simply asked Lot to take whichever part he wanted in the land ...

> *And there was strife between the herdsmen of Abram's livestock and the herdsmen of Lot's livestock. The Canaanites and the Perizzites then dwelt in the land. So Abram said to Lot, "Please let there be no strife between you and me, and between my herdsmen and your herdsmen; for we are brethren. Is not the whole land before you? Please separate from me. If you take the left, then I will go to the right; or, if you go to the right, then I will go to the left.*
>
> *(Genesis 13:7-9)*

Perhaps this describes who you are as a person, and you have tried so much to change yourself because you feel people always take advantage of you. My humble suggestion is that you should embrace who you are with joy and begin to look for opportunities to use this unique nature for God and for His glory.

4. **THE BALANCED ONES:** As the name connotes, these are people with a broad, balanced, conscientious, and analytical personality. They tend to be incredibly detailed, tidy, and focused. They are also called Investigators and are very orderly, thorough, and also very precise. They are usually very thoughtful and discerning, and like everything being kept in its place. They

do things in a systematic way and always like to be well prepared for events and functions they have to feature in.

These set of people are also highly organized and are the type who like people returning things to the exact place where they take things from. They tend to be very petty and particular about such things! Yours sincerely who happens to fall into this group, used to have a lot of problems with this issue at the home front. I would nag members of my family (including my 'poor' husband) about why things should always be returned to the exact position where they were taken from, facing the exact direction where I had placed them! Yes, it was that bad! I was to later realize that the fact that I had been *wired* this way did not mean everybody around me saw things the way I did!

The downside of the Investigators is that they tend to be too suspicious, finicky, compulsive and always want to be perfectionists (which is usually impossible). They also often have unrealistic expectations for themselves and people around them. As a result of this, they might frustrate the people around them. This group of people also find it difficult handling sudden changes, as they always like being prepared before taking up any task. They usually do excellently well as Writers, Designers, Accountants, Lawyers, Administrators, and the likes.

Joseph was someone with a conscientious personality. He was a highly organized and thorough person and manifested this when he was a slave in the household of Potiphar and when he was sent to prison.

*And his master saw that the LORD was with him and that the LORD made all he did to prosper in his hand. So Joseph found favor in his sight, and served him. Then he made him overseer of his house, and all that he had he put under his authority. So it was, from the time that he had*

**Balanced and detailed!**

*made him overseer of his house and all that he had, that the LORD blessed the Egyptian's house for Joseph's sake; and the blessing of the LORD was on all that he had in the house and in the field. Thus he left all that he had in Joseph's hand, and he did not know what he had, except for the bread which he ate. Now Joseph was handsome in form and appearance.*

**(Genesis 39:2-6)**

As was mentioned earlier, it is very possible to have a combination of qualities from at least two personality types. However, the traits of a particular type will be more dominant than the other. This however does not change the fact that as a person, you have a combination unique to you.

Having read through the description of each personality type, you need to take time to discover your personality type, your strengths, and weaknesses. There are a lot of good tests that are available online which you can take within a few minutes, and which will generate results for you. Some of them are free and for some, you might have to pay a small amount to access. You can do a good search on your Google search engine and pick one or two that you find suitable.

Taking these tests will give you a quick grasp of your personality type. It is also a good idea to read more about these personality tests.

However, whatever your personality type is, begin to celebrate your strengths and use them for God's glory. Thereafter, you need to submit your weaknesses to the Lord and to the transforming power of the Holy Spirit, in humility and in the place of prayers.

**Now, take time to fill out these spaces ...**

> **I believe my personality type is**_____

➤ **Therefore, I am** _____, _____ **and**
_____ (*List out three qualities of your personality type that best describe you*).

➤ **My strengths are**_____, _____
**and** _____

(*List out three strong values that best describe you*)

➤ **With the help of the Holy Spirit, I will work on the following weaknesses:**_____, _____
**and** _____

(*List out three weak points that you believe best describe you*)
**So help me, God.**

# CHAPTER TEN

# You Have A Passion For Something

*"Passion is energy. Feel the power that comes from focusing on what excites you."*
**(Oprah Winfrey)**

Everyone is passionate about something; everyone has a passion for something. Your passion is simply that thing you really love to do or to talk about. It determines what your affections, ambitions, hopes, and aspirations are. God has given every one of us the enthusiasm and love for something. Some people have the passion for taking care of children, the sick, the elderly or even animals. There is a reason why God gives some people passion or a burden for something and others an interest in something else. This is because the passion in a person's heart is a pointer to the problem, he or she has been created by God to solve.

Therefore, it will be foolhardy to try to copy what somebody else is doing, just because the person seems to be succeeding in it! We have many stories from history, of people who made great impact on their generations, just because they paid attention to the passions in their heart. The stories of these three great women come to mind …

1. **Florence Nightingale**: Born into a wealthy English family, she grew up in a privileged family in the days when rich women did not have to work, but would sit all day around a table, taking tea and biscuits, socializing, and gossiping. She was also expected to marry early, but she had other desires. As she grew up, she became passionate about helping the poor and the sick and her heart was always drawn to neighborhoods where they lived. To the disappointment of her influential family, she decided to become a nurse. At that time, nursing was not seen as a profession and nurses did not have a good reputation. They were seen as dirty and inconsequential.

However, Florence went on to change the face of nursing worldwide by introducing processes and procedures that made the practice of the profession safer and healthier for patients. The impact of this was particularly noticeable in 1854 during the Crimean War, where she had led a group of nurses to care for soldiers hurt in the war. Their healthy practices had greatly reduced the death rate of the patients. She continued to pour her heart and life into making nursing an honorable and well-respected profession. By the time she died, she had written over 150 books and many other resources that addressed health issues. Today, the story of nursing is incomplete without the name of Florence Nightingale being mentioned.[1]

2. **Mary Slessor:** She was raised in abject poverty, and experienced the tragedy of losing her father, brothers and later her mother and sister. However, she refused to be weighed down by the tragic events she had experienced and was hopeful about securing a more glorious future by going into missions.

This was at a time when it was mainly men who were considered for missionary work. Mary lost her elder brother who was also planning to become a missionary. Shortly after this, she also heard about the death of a famous missionary and explorer called David Livingstone. These two events made Mary decide to become a missionary and she applied for the post.

In 1875, at the age of 27, she was accepted and sent as a missionary by the United Presbyterian Church of Scotland to Calabar in the southeastern part of Nigeria in West Africa. She lived amongst the people, learnt to speak the native Efik language and learnt about the culture of the people. She was to later discover a heartbreaking and disturbing trend in the land, which was the killing of twin babies as soon as they were born! The native people believed that it was an abomination for a woman to give birth to twins, whom they felt had been fathered by an evil spirit! As a result of this, twin babies were killed, and their mothers ostracized from the society.

Mary decided to do something about this and stood her ground in the fight against this evil practice, at the risk of losing her life. She saw this as a divine mandate and was extremely passionate about it. Her major desire was for twin babies, who were either killed or left to die due to the idolatrous practices and beliefs of the people, to be rescued. Eventually, she found favor with the people, gained their respect, and had great success with the abolition of the killing of twins. She rescued many of these babies, brought them up and adopted many of them.

By the time she died in 1925 about 40 years after she arrived in Calabar, she had been instrumental to the eradication of many other superstitious beliefs in the communities where she lived. Despite series of bouts of illnesses during the 40 years she spent in Nigeria, Mary Slessor persevered. By the time she died at the age of 66, she left a legacy impossible to erase from the minds of the Calabar people of southern Nigeria.[2]

3. **Harriet Tubman**- She was born a slave around 1820 but made up her mind that she would not die as a slave. She grew up in a large family with ten brothers and sisters. They all lived and worked for many long hours as slaves on a plantation, laboring in fields of corn, potatoes, and tobacco. As she watched her parents, siblings and friends work long and hard hours in the fields from morning till evening, and she saw many of them being beaten, she began to dream of a better life for herself and her family.

In her twenties, she got married to a free African American man called John Tubman. This did not however change her status, as she remained a slave because her owner could decide to sell her to someone else at any time. Harriet began to plan her escape and discussed this with her husband, who did not like the idea. She eventually convinced her brothers to escape to freedom with her, but they decided to turn back as they embarked on the journey.

Without any one to support her, Harriet Tubman escaped from the Brodess Plantation in Maryland to the city of Philadelphia in the northern part of America. She had walked for almost one hundred miles to freedom! Even as a free person, Harriet was not satisfied, as she also longed to see members of her family being free. Her passion was for the liberation of as many black slaves as possible. She then returned to the plantation where she had lived in Maryland, to help them escape to freedom.

She helped her parents and many of her brothers and sisters and their families to escape into the northern part of the country through what has become known as the Underground Railroad. They would travel by night and rest during the day. Not only that, she also made a total of nineteen trips to the southern part of the nation over a period of ten years, to help over three hundred other slaves escape into freedom!

Later in her life, during the American Civil War, she worked for the Union Army as a cook, nurse and then a spy. At a time, she led a civil war raid which helped to free more than 700 slaves in

South Carolina! Harriet became known as the Moses of her people. She spent the rest of her life caring for the old, sick, and poor and continued to fight for the rights of women. By the time she died in 1920 at the age of 93, she had received many honors and had become an incredibly famous and highly respected American. She is remembered as a former slave who risked her life to win her freedom and the freedom of others. She continues to be an inspiration to women and men alike all over the world. So much for someone born a slave![3]

What are you passionate about? What do you love to think or talk about the most? What stirs and arouses your interest? What makes you cry or burdens you the most? For Nelson Mandela, it was to see the end of apartheid; for Martin Luther King Jr, it was to see the end of segregation. For Moses in the Bible, it was to see the deliverance of his people from the bondage of the Egyptians. What cause are you ready to die for? You need to discover what you are passionate about and spend the rest of your life pursuing it.

**As you ponder in your heart what exactly your passion might be, I encourage you to take time to answer the following questions. I believe they will help you begin the process of identifying your passion**

1.  **What is the deepest desire of my heart?**

    _____

    _____

2.  **What do I love to think or talk about the most?**

    _____

    _____

3.  **What stirs and arouses my interest?**

    _____

    _____

4. What makes me cry or burdens me the most?

_____

_____

**MY PASSION(S) IS (ARE)**

_____

_____

# CHAPTER ELEVEN

# You Have Some Hidden Potentials

*"Inside every human being, there are treasures to unlock."*

**(Mike Huckabee)**

In his book, ***Understanding Your Potential***,[1] Dr. Myles Munroe describes Potential as "Dormant and Capped Ability, Reserved Power, Untapped Strength, Unused Success, Unexposed Ability, Latent Power and Hidden Talents."

Your potentials are therefore the unique make-up of your natural abilities, gifts and talents. They are abilities that are inherent in you from birth and need to be 'unwrapped,' developed and used for God's glory. They are the treasures that are lying dormant inside you and need to be unearthed. The truth is that all of us have at least one talent that has been uniquely placed in us by God to help us fulfill His assignment for us here on earth. It can be the ability to sing, to write, to dance, to draw … the list is endless. These are natural abilities we possess and did not learn anywhere.

A particularly good example of this is found in the book of Exodus 31: 1-5 ...

> *Then the LORD spoke to Moses, saying: "See, I have called by name Bezaleel the son of Uri, the son of Hur, of the tribe of Judah. And I have filled him with the Spirit of God, in wisdom, in understanding, in knowledge, and in all manner of workmanship, to design artistic works, to work in gold, in silver, in bronze, in cutting jewels for setting, in carving wood, and to work in all manner of workmanship."*
>
> *(Exodus 31:1-5)*

God had given Moses the design of the tabernacle which He wanted him to build for Him. God then told Moses that He had also specially gifted Bezaleel and Aholiab to help him in this assignment through the manifestation of their creative gifts and natural abilities.

Likewise, dear friend, your gift or talent has been given to you by God so that you can use it for the expansion of His work. In essence, a talent from God is given to you to make the world a better place and not to torment, afflict and oppress others. The world is filled with people (some of whom were probably not Christians) who discovered their talents, developed them, and used them to make the world a better place. People like Walt Disney, founder of Disney Land, Michelangelo, the famous sculptor and painter, music composer Beethoven; singers and song writers Donnie McClurkin and Don Moen, among many others.

The parable of the talents, as told by the Lord Jesus Christ, gives a clearer picture of this ...

> *For the kingdom of heaven is like a man traveling to a far country, who called his own servants and delivered his goods to them. And to one he*

*gave five talents, to another two, and to another one, to each according to his own ability; and immediately he went on a journey. Then he who had received the five talents went and traded with money. After a long time, the lord of those servants came and settled accounts them, and made another five talents. And likewise, he who had received two gained two more also. But he who had received one went and dug in the ground and hid his lord's with them.*

*(Matthew 25: 14-19)*

In the above passage, Jesus shared the story of a man who, as he prepared for a long trip, gave talents to each of his servants in different measures. He gave one of them five talents, to another he gave two and the last one he gave one. The Bible says in the book of Matthew 25:14-19 that the master gave each of them the amount he did, based on their abilities. Likewise, God gives us gifts and talents based on the way He has *wired* us, and what He knows we can handle. It will therefore be out of place to compare ourselves with others or to be envious of what they have or what they can do.

On his return, the master asked each of them to give an account of what they had done with their talents. The ones who had received five and two talents had doubled theirs, while the one who had received one talent did nothing with his! Rather, he had hidden it in the ground! This got the master angry, and he collected the single talent he had and gave it to the one who had increased his own to ten talents. He then made some pronouncements on the servant, which we could consider a bit harsh, but portrays how serious this matter is to God.

*But his lord answered and said to him, 'You wicked and lazy servant, you knew that I reap where I have not sown and gather where I have not scattered seed. So you ought to have deposited my money with the bankers, and at my coming I would have received back my own with interest. Therefore take the talent from him, and give it to him who has ten talents. 'For to everyone who has, more will be given, and he will have abundance; but from him who does not have, even what he has will be taken away. And cast the unprofitable servant into the outer darkness. There will be weeping and gnashing of teeth.*

*(Matthew 25:26-30)*

This unfortunately describes the state of many of us. We simply conclude that because what we have been given does not appear as important as what others have, it cannot be useful or productive and then we simply hide or bury it. This is usually because we are limited in our knowledge of our Master – the giver of the gifts.

The servant with the one talent spoke to his master …

*Then he who had received the one talent came and said, 'Lord, I knew you to be a hard man, reaping where you have not sown, and gathering where you have not scattered seed. And I was afraid and went and hid your talent in the ground. Look, there you have what is yours.*

*(Matthew 25:24-25)*

His perception of his master was what determined what he did with his talent. He saw his master as hard, wicked, and selfish. He failed to realize that the talent had been given to him to trade with. He failed to realize that the talent was given to him to use and to multiply. He also allowed fear to grip his heart and to hinder him from moving forward. He became an unfruitful tree that was just taking up space.

The truth is this:

You are loaded, very well packaged, and well put together by God Almighty Himself. Every one of us has at least one talent which, as we put it to use, will multiply. You are not a piece of junk, trash, or a good-for-nothing person. You have been placed on this earth to unearth your talent(s), your hidden treasures, and your potentials. It is your responsibility to discover them and use them to glorify God.

The sad thing, however, is that many times we walk around in ignorance, simply because we do not know whose we are, who we are and what we have. This ought not to be so.

What then are these treasures, and how then do we unearth them?

A treasure is that thing of value that God has placed inside you, which, when it is 'mined' and brought out of you, will take you to places far beyond your imagination. I believe that some of the greatest treasures and assets we possess are the talents, gifts and unique abilities God gave to us.

Many times, people complain that they do not know what to do with their lives, what business to go into, or what career to pursue. Many are confused and seem to have no direction. However, once they discover that God has placed something inside them that needs to be 'mined' and unearthed, which represents their gateway to success, influence and even wealth, the story changes. This, dear friend is my desire and prayer for you, as you read this book.

**How then do we unearth these treasures and talents?**

➢ **It begins with God** – If we believe that God has uniquely packaged each one of us, He is the best person to ask the question. This we should do in the place of intense and heartfelt prayers. He has promised us in the book of Isaiah.

*I will give you the treasures of darkness, and the hidden riches of secret places, that you may know that I the Lord, who call you by your name, am the God of Israel.*

*(Isaiah 45:3)*

Therefore, ask God to open your eyes to see all the treasures He has placed inside you, so that you can use them for His glory.

- ➤ **Do your research** – This is the time for you to do your research and take time to study yourself. There is a list of useful questions that can help you with this at the end of this chapter. Ask yourself these simple but direct questions and the answers will amaze you! You will discover that there are some abilities you possess, which you have not paid attention to. They could be the ability to write, sing, dance, act, cook, organize, play a musical instrument etc. The list goes on and on.
- ➤ **Ask people close to you** – You can also ask trusted people who know you well. Many people close to us can help us identify things they have noticed over the years, that we do very well. (A note of caution however: Do not be discouraged if people you feel should know you well, do not seem to have anything positive to tell you. Just take your attention away from such people).
- ➤ **Be sincere with yourself, and do not overlook anything** – No treasure or gift is too small for God to use for His glory. Remember, the ability of Joseph to interpret dreams took him to the very top as prime minister of Egypt – the most powerful nation in the world at that time. Also, it was the lunch box of a young boy that the Lord Jesus Christ used to feed five thousand people …

*One of His disciples, Andrew, Simon Peter's brother, said to Him, "There is a lad here who has five barley loaves and two small fish, but what are they among so many?" Then Jesus said, "Make the people sit down." Now there was much grass in the place. So the men sat down, in number about five thousand. And Jesus took the loaves, and when He had given thanks He distributed them to the disciples, and the disciples to those sitting down; and likewise of the fish, as much as they wanted. So when they were filled, He said to His disciples, "Gather up the fragments that remain, so that nothing is lost." Therefore they gathered them up, and filled twelve baskets with the fragments of the five barley loaves which were left over by those who had eaten. Then those men, when they had seen the sign that Jesus did, said, "This is truly the Prophet who is to come into the world."*

**(John 6:8-14)**

The moment you unearth your treasures, there are some things you should start doing. You need to begin to polish your treasure, because it is usually given to you in a raw state.

I recently came across a quote by a famous Scottish preacher, Late Rev. Thomas Guthrie[2] that says, *"The more the diamond is cut, the brighter it sparkles..."*

In essence, what brings out the true beauty of a gemstone is the tough processing it goes through – the cutting, the filling and in some instances, the heating.

I also recall someone showing me a piece of raw gold many years ago. It looked very rough and unattractive. However, if that same piece of gold is put in fire, you would be amazed at what would come out!

Likewise, your treasure (gift, talent, and ability) when unearthed, is in a raw state and needs to be refined by going through some processing, to bring out its absolute best. This might involve you going back to school, attending some trainings, or simply serving under the tutelage of someone more experienced than you.

Understandably, this might be a very humbling experience, but it will be worth it. I encourage you to take time to polish that treasure and let it sparkle and shine, to the glory of God.

**Now, let us take a look at these questions ...**
**Questions to ask yourself:**

1.  **What do I love to do?**

_____

_____

_____

2.  **What can I do effortlessly without getting tired?**

_____

_____

_____

3.  **What am I willing to do, even if no one pays me for it?**

_____

_____

_____

4.  **What have people around me told me I am good at?**

_____

_____

_____

5. **What can I do well that I did not learn anywhere?**

_____

_____

_____

## MY POTENTIALS ARE

_____

_____

# CHAPTER TWELVE

# Your Past Experiences Matter

*"Turn your scars into stars."*

**(Robert Schuller)**

We are all products of the experiences we have had in our lives. Experiences are circumstances that have come your way in life, some of which were beyond your control, but have molded you. These include Family, Education, Spiritual and Painful Experiences. Many times, God allows us to go through some difficult moments and challenges because of the assignment He has for us. It could also be because of a problem He wants us to solve here on Earth.

Do you know that you cannot really give what you do not have? Likewise, you cannot share from an encounter you have not personally experienced. This is why, for instance, it is only a woman that has had delay in conception and childbirth that can give a heartfelt counsel to a woman who is going through the same challenge. Likewise, it is only a woman that has either experienced a failed marriage, widowhood, a life-threatening disease, raised a challenged child and has come out victorious, that can truly counsel others who are in a similar situation.

Therefore, I encourage you not to give up in the face of the challenges you are facing at present. I urge you to be strong in the Lord and in the power of His might. That situation will surely end in praise, in Jesus name.

> *Finally, my brethren, be strong in the Lord and in the power of His might.*
>
> *(Ephesians 6:10)*

While encouraging women who are passing through challenges, I usually tell them that the test or trial that comes their way is not just about them, but because of others coming after them, who will need to hear their success stories. There are so many examples out there to confirm this.

Today, celebrated preacher and award-winning author, Joyce Meyer's story, is seen as a source of encouragement to any woman who has been a victim of any form of abuse. Just as she has mentioned on several occasions, Joyce experienced sexual abuse at the hands of her biological father for many years. She had grown up broken, bitter, and battered, until she met the Lord Jesus Christ, who transformed her life. Today, she is a powerful vessel in God's hand, helping women to deal with emotional challenges, as she leads them to find healing in the hands of the 'Balm of Gilead.'

Pastor Rick Warren also notes in his book, *Purpose Driven Life*, that **"God does not waste anything."** Every challenge people go through in life is working out for a greater good ...

> *And we know that all things work together for good to those who love God, to those who are called according to His purpose.*
>
> **(Romans 8:28)**

What lessons did you learn while growing up? What have you had to deal with, while growing up? What problems, hurts, thorns, and disappointments have you experienced in the past? Did you grow up in a dysfunctional and abusive family? Were you abused in any way? As you grew up, did you have to deal with lack, poverty, and loss? Were your parents divorced or separated? Did you fail at school?

TV personality, Oprah Winfrey, has not always been the success that she is today. According to her, while growing up, she experienced sexual abuse in the hands of some relatives and even had a child at the age of 14, which she sadly lost. Today, she has found purpose in helping people tell their stories and overcome their pains and hurts through her various media platforms.

Taking a cue from the Bible, we also see from the life of Moses that it was the same wilderness that he had passed through 40 years before (when he fled from Pharaoh) that God now asked him to take the children of Israel through, when they left Egypt.

> *Now therefore, behold, the cry of the children of Israel has come to Me, and I have also seen the oppression with which the Egyptians oppress them. Come now, therefore, and I will send you to Pharaoh, that you may bring My people, the children of Israel, out of Egypt.*
>
> *(Exodus 3:9-10)*

What you are going through at present is a preparation ground for a bigger and better assignment in your future.

Some unpleasant situations I experienced while growing up caused me a lot of emotional pain as a young girl. As I grew up, I saw my mother experience all forms of emotional, physical, and financial abuse and she had to deal with the trauma of all these while still raising her six children and building her career as a high school teacher. I saw her experience depths of lack amid plenty, such that there were times she would ask me to lend her some money out of my college allowance, just to keep body and soul together! I witnessed my mother cry on several occasions as she bore the weight of the abuse.

Some years after, when she surrendered her life to Christ, I saw how, with her newfound faith, she received strength to handle the pressures at the home front. I saw firsthand how she later experienced a turnaround in her life and finances, the moment she focused on what she was passionate about, which was teaching.

To the glory of God, this same woman went on to start two schools that have become award-winning centers of education in her home state. She is now an employer of labor, feeding multitudes daily and being used of God to mentor and train many others, as a preacher and teacher of the Word. These things that I saw and experienced while growing up, stirred in me the burden and the passion to help women I meet in my lifetime, to discover purpose and to become economically strong.

You see, as I mentioned in the preface to this book, I also experienced what I call the "wilderness season" of my life. Though I got married shortly after I left college to a wonderful child of God, I still did not find lasting joy in my heart as it relates to my career. I graduated at the top of my class, but I studied a course that I was not exactly passionate about. When I started working, I hated every moment of it. Monday mornings were always a nightmare for me as I dreaded having to sit through work for another week. Eventually, I resigned from my job and took time to find out what I wanted to focus on. I then entered a season of despair, frustration and near depression for about ten years. I was confused and disillusioned. I could not understand why I hated going to work every Monday morning. Was I just being lazy? Was I out of my mind? Why did I have this sense of dissatisfaction? So many questions were on my mind at that time. However, I knew deep down within me that there was certainly something better for me out there.

Later on, after a season of intense self-reflection, study of the

Word, research by reading books, messages, heartfelt prayers and also by simply being observant, God showed up! He opened my eyes to help me discover who I really am. I discovered that I am a unique being, specially created by God to fulfill a unique purpose. He helped me to unearth my hidden treasures! I would rather say He opened my eyes to see the treasures that had been in me all the while. Right from a young age, I had always loved writing and speaking. I also had a flair for planning events. However, I never saw them as anything special, until I realized it was not everyone who enjoyed doing these things! I knew some people who considered these skills a nightmare! I then realized that they are my own special gifts and talents given to me by God.

I then decided to focus on the things I loved doing, which I could do effortlessly. I went back to postgraduate school at the age of 42 and obtained a master's degree in media and communication, to sharpen my skill as a communicator. During the program, I was pregnant with my last child, gave birth to him during the course and was back in class exactly two weeks after his delivery! Talk about passion!

I also went on to build capacity as a professional trainer and became certified by the International Training Centre of International Labor Organization (ILO) a United Nations (UN) agency. Today, my career path is centered around writing, speaking, teaching, and training, which I absolutely love! I now have a level of self-confidence and personal fulfillment, doing what I am passionate about and I am reaping the financial rewards to the glory of God.

Dear friend: Your breakthrough lies in the place of your assignment and purpose.

Furthermore, the lessons I learnt during this season of my life, coupled with the ones I witnessed at the home front while growing up, were the genesis of the formation of **The Women of Essence Foundation,** an organization set up to help women to discover, pursue and fulfil purpose. The organization is now in its ninth year and it has been involved in various initiatives in the empowerment of women and girls, since inception.

As we end this chapter, please bear in mind that everything you have gone through (or you are going through) is an indication of the problems God has sent you to solve here on Earth. Therefore, I encourage you to forget about your past and free your heart of every form of offence and bitterness you might have experienced as a result of what you went through in the past. The glory that is ahead of you is far greater than the pains of the past.

➢ **Let your past become a launching pad for your future**
➢ **Let your misery become your ministry**
➢ **Let your curse become your cause**
➢ **Let your pain become your gain**

As you do this, you are on your way to a great and a glorious future!!

God bless you!

**FOR PERSONAL REFLECTION**
Now, take time to answer these questions ...

1. What issues did I have to deal with, while growing up?

_____

_____

_____

2. What lessons did I learn, while growing up?

_____

_____

_____

3. What problems, hurts, thorns, and disappointments have I experienced in the past?

_____

_____

_____

4. What challenges have I overcome in life that I can encourage others with?

_____

_____

_____

## MY FIVE PETALS DIAGRAM

Now that you have gone through the second part of this book, please fill the space in each petal in the picture below …

I am a unique being. My **FIVE** petals make me unique as follows …

Now that you have been able to articulate your 5Ps, let us move on to the next chapter.

# PART THREE
## After Discovery, What Next?

# CHAPTER THIRTEEN

# Embrace And Celebrate Your Uniqueness

*Now faith is the substance of things hoped for, the evidence of things not seen.*

*(Hebrews11:1)*

In the last section, we looked at the components of Personal Discovery, which I referred to as the "**Five Petals of Personal Discovery.**™ They are ...

- ➤ Physical Appearance
- ➤ Personality
- ➤ Passion
- ➤ Potentials and
- ➤ Past Experiences.

We noted that everyone has a unique combination of all these components that are peculiar to each person. I hope you have been able to fill out all the dotted lines in the questions at the end of each chapter.

Do not get discouraged if you do not have all the answers now. As you begin to take some necessary and intentional steps, many things about your life will become clearer to you. You see, sometimes, God simply waits for us to take the first steps before He begins to show more things to us. When God first called Abraham in Genesis 12:1-2, He only gave him a promise of greatness.

> *Now the LORD had said to Abram:*
> *Get out of your country,*
> *From your family,*
> *And from your father's house,*
> *To a land that I will show you. I will make you a great nation;*
> *I will bless you,*
> *And make your name great;*
> *And you shall be a blessing. I will bless those who bless you,*
> *And I will curse him who curses you;*
> *And in you all the families of the earth shall be blessed.*

**(Genesis 12:1-3)**

It was after Abraham heeded the call that God began to give him more information and specific details about Isaac –the son and child of promise that was to come.

> *After these things the word of the LORD came to Abram in a vision, saying, 'Do not be afraid, Abram. I am your shield, your exceedingly great reward.' But Abram said, "Lord GOD, what will You give me, seeing I go childless, and the heir of my house is Eliezer of Damascus?" Then Abram said, "Look, You have given me no offspring; indeed one born in my house is my heir!" And behold, the word of the LORD came to him, saying, "This one shall not be your heir, but one who will come from your own body shall be your heir,"*

*Then He brought him outside and said, "Look now toward heaven, and count the stars if you are able to number them." And He said to him, 'So shall your descendants be.*

*(Genesis 15:1-5)*

For every step of faith that we take, God backs us up and gives more insight and direction. Now that you have a clearer picture of who you are as a person, the next question is –**What next?**

➢ First, you need to take time to understand your 5Ps. This might involve doing more research either by reading more books on the subject or asking relevant questions. At the back of this book is a list of good books about Self Discovery that you can also take time to read. You can also invest in some good biographies and read about the lives of some successful people who followed their passion. Find out why they succeeded and why they failed. The Bible is also filled with true life stories of different types of people that we can learn a lot of lessons from.

➢ Afterwards, you need to begin to celebrate your uniqueness, not in a proud or arrogant manner, but in a way that will bring glory to God. Understand that you have been created by God to fulfill a unique purpose which will make you a blessing to your generation. Never make the mistake of comparing yourself with others, wishing you could be someone else. The best you can be of another person is a copy. You can only be the best version of yourself.

➢ Likewise, never look down on others because you seem more gifted or more talented than them. God has given us what He knows we can handle and what will be needed in the fulfillment of our destinies. In the 'Parable of Talents,' as told by The Lord Jesus Christ, each person was given a measure of talent based on his own ability.

*And to one he gave five talents, to another two, and to another one, to each according to his own ability; and immediately he went on a journey.*

**(Matthew 25:15)**

➤ Accept the way you have been *wired* by God and celebrate your uniqueness. Begin to walk with the consciousness that you are a blessing and a solution to the world. See yourself as a unique person on a unique assignment.

- Accept your uniqueness.
- Believe it, and
- Confess it!

**I encourage you to make this confession right now …**

- *I am a **unique** being specially packaged by God to fulfill a **unique** assignment.*
- *I am of the right height, right size, right shape and I have the right skin colour. They are all part of what makes me unique.*
- *I have inside me, unique gifts, talents and abilities that God has placed there to help me fulfill my purpose.*
- *This is why I love to do the things I do, and I love to talk about the things I talk about.*
- *My **purpose** is beyond my position or any title I might ever hold.*
- *I can only find true fulfilment when I operate the way I have been wired by God.*
- I *Thank God for who I am!*
- I *Thank God for my glorious destiny!*

I am unique!

# CHAPTER FOURTEEN

# Get Rid Of Limiting Beliefs

*...for as a man thinks in his heart, so is he*
**(Proverbs 23:7)**

The heart is an immensely powerful part of the human body. The moment the heart stops beating, one can easily conclude that the person concerned has passed on. However, the word "heart" is also used to describe the unseen part of a person which controls the emotions, thoughts, feelings, desires and intellect. Sometimes, it is used interchangeably with the word "mind" in the Bible.

Your heart or mind is the core of your being. It is to you what the CPU – the central processing unit, is to the computer. The information that the computer is fed with, goes into its CPU, and this information is displayed on the computer monitor. As they say "garbage in, garbage out."

Likewise, the mind or heart which is like the human CPU, receives, processes, stores and displays any information that it is fed with, through the gates of the heart. These gates are the five senses of Sight, Sound, Smell, Taste, and Touch. The processed information is then expressed through human actions, words, and deeds. The information that is stored in the heart then develops into a set of beliefs that settle in the mind of the person concerned.

The quality of information you receive and process in your mind, determines the quality of your actions, your words, and your deeds. No wonder the Bible says in Proverbs 23:7, that what a man repeatedly thinks about himself will eventually become his reality. Many people are bound by the lies they have embraced about themselves and their situations, over time. As a result of this, they are unable to rise above their present circumstances, except they do something about these lies. These lies are called **limiting beliefs,** which hinder us from pursuing the dreams we have in our hearts and the assignment that God has for us.

Motivational speaker and author Brian Tracy puts it well when he said, "*You begin to fly when you let go of self-limiting beliefs and allow your mind and aspirations to rise to greater heights.*"[1]

As children of God, it is therefore necessary to deal with the limiting beliefs in our hearts (minds). We must embrace the truth of God's Word and reject every falsehood that the enemy of our soul has sold to us. This is why the Word of God tells us in Romans 12:1-2 to be transformed in the way we think …

The Bible tells us in Romans 12: 1-2, what to do with the mind …

*I beseech you therefore, brethren, by the mercies of God, that you present your bodies a living sacrifice, holy, acceptable to God, which is your reasonable service. And do not be conformed to this world, but be transformed by the renewing of your mind, that you may prove what is that good and acceptable and perfect will of God.*

**(Romans 12:1-2)**

Moses is one person in the Bible who had embraced a lot of limiting beliefs about himself. The Lord appeared to Moses in the burning bush and told him the great assignment that He wanted Moses to accomplish for Him. Moses tried to convince God that he was not the right person for the assignment.

He asked God several questions which reflected the state of his heart and the limiting beliefs he had about himself …

*But Moses said to God, "Who am I that I should go to Pharaoh, and that I should bring the children of Israel out of Egypt?" So He said, "I will certainly be with you. And this shall be a sign to you that I have sent you: When you have brought the people out of Egypt, you shall serve God on this mountain." Then Moses said to God, "Indeed, when I come to the children of Israel and say to them, 'The God of your fathers has sent me to you,' and they say to me, 'What is His name?' what shall I say to them?*

One would wonder why Moses who had been raised as a prince in Egypt would ask these types of questions. What could have happened to him over the years since the time he fled from Egypt as a fugitive? It is obvious that the 40 years he had spent in the wilderness living and working with his father-in-law as a shepherd must have battered his self-image. He spoke like someone who had a low self-esteem.

Despite the several reassurances that God gave Moses, he still responded to God with these words …

*O my Lord, I am not eloquent, neither before nor since You have spoken to Your servant; but I am slow of speech and slow of tongue. So the LORD said to him, "Who has made man's mouth? Or who makes the mute, the deaf, the seeing, or the blind? Have not I, the LORD? Now therefore, go, and I will be with your mouth and teach you what you shall say. But he said, "O my Lord, please send by the hand of whomever else You may send."*

**(Exodus 4:10-13)**

Thankfully, God helped Moses overcome all these fears by assuring him yet again of His divine presence and enablement. He also gave him the tool through which he would fulfill his assignment and perform great signs and wonders- **THE ROD!** The same rod he had been carrying around for years, to lead and guide the sheep in his custody!

Likewise, do you know that God has already placed in your hands and in your life "the rod" you will use to do exploits for Him?

Your 5Ps (Five Petals) as discussed in the last section of this book are the things that make up your rod. It is time to pick up this rod and begin to use it for God's glory. Halleluyah!

> *Now you shall speak to him and put the words in his mouth. And I will be with your mouth and with his mouth, and I will teach you what you shall do. So he shall be your spokesman to the people. And he himself shall be as a mouth for you, and you shall be to him as God. And you shall take this rod in your hand, with which you shall do the signs.*

**(Exodus 4:15-17)**

However, Moses himself and the rod in his hands had to go through a process of transformation before they could become tools in God's hands. Your gifts, talents and all other things that make up your 5Ps must be surrendered to God with the promise to use them only for His glory. Why? There is always the tendency for us to begin to feel self-reliant and arrogant when we start getting outstanding results through our rods. We must deal with pride and arrogance in our lives.

After the encounter Moses had with God, his rod was later referred to as **THE ROD OF GOD,** as he left for Egypt.

> *Then Moses took his wife and his sons and set them on a donkey, and he returned to the land of Egypt. And Moses took the rod of God in his hand.*
>
> **(Exodus4:20)**

As we conclude this chapter, it is necessary to take time to reflect on some self-limiting beliefs that you might have embraced about yourself over time. This could be as a result of your background, your upbringing, your lack of qualifications, your race, your tribe, your skin colour and so on.

Perhaps you are already asking yourself these same questions that Moses asked ...

- Who am I?
- What do I have?
- Who do I know?
- What will I say?
- What if they do not believe me?

And much more

You have probably also given yourself a million reasons why you cannot fulfill your purpose or attain anything great in life. Reasons such as ...

- I am not good enough
- I cannot speak well
- I have an accent
- I am not well-educated
- No one in my family has ever done this before ...

What does God's Word say about you? What does the Word of God say you can do and that you can have? You need to embrace God's truth as your truth! It is time to challenge and drop all these limiting beliefs, and to embrace the Word of God!

*I encourage you to take this short exercise ...*
1. Write down a list of limiting beliefs you have had to deal with in your life

   _____

   _____

2. How have these beliefs affected your life?

   _____

   _____

3. Take a look at these Bible passages and highlight how they address the beliefs listed in question one above.
   - **Jeremiah 1:5**

     _____

     _____

   - **Jeremiah 29:11**

     _____

     _____

   - **Psalm139:13-14**

     _____

     _____

   - **Philippians 4:13**

     _____

     _____

# CHAPTER FIFTEEN

## Look Out For Opportunites To Serve

*"When you focus on being a blessing, God makes sure that you are always blessed in abundance."*

**(Joel Osteen)**

The moment you have an idea of what you love doing, what you have a passion for, and what your gifts and talents are, the best thing to do is to begin to look for opportunities to serve, using your **5Ps.** It is such a blessing to be a source of joy to someone else. It is a greater blessing to give of what you have to others, than to receive. In the words of Paul the Apostle …

> *I have shown you in every way, by laboring like this, that you must support the weak. And remember the words of the Lord Jesus, that He said, "It is more blessed to give than to receive."*
>
> **(Acts20:35)**

Another good thing is that the more you put your resources and treasures to use, the more you get better at what you do. As long as a treasure remains beneath the earth's surface, it will remain untapped, dormant and useless. Therefore, as you discover what your potentials and gifts are, begin to look out for opportunities to put them to use. Do not let money be your motivation. Rather, let your motivation be your desire to help other people solve problems with the use of your gifts. Notable author and speaker, Brian Tracy said this of successful people ...

*"...Successful people are always looking for opportunities to help others. Unsuccessful people are always asking, 'What's in it for me?'"*

To begin with, you can look for places or organizations where you can volunteer and offer free services. I tell people that the best place to do this is in their local assembly or fellowship. Go and "sow" to God the treasure of your gifts and talents in His house and wait to see how He will open unimaginable doors for you. He is forever faithful!

Do you know that some of the experiences you have gone through and overcame in life will be an encouragement to someone else? I know a lady who lost her husband at a young age and was left with young children to care for. Today, she reaches out to widows like herself, encouraging and strengthening them with her success story, having been helped by God to raise outstanding children.

When you give of your time and resources to others, and you do it cheerfully, you can never diminish in life. You cannot quantify the blessings that you get when you see what you do effortlessly, bring joy to another person. This is what made a young Albanian lady called Agnes Gonxha Bojaxhiu to leave her family and devote her entire life to the care of the sick and extremely poor in India. This young lady was Mother Theresa[1] of blessed memory. She never got married and had no biological children of her own, by the time she died. However, at her burial, the whole nation of India literally stood still, to celebrate the life of this great woman. Presidents of nations attended her burial ceremony. A life of service will always command greater blessings and honor.

When you wake up each day of your life, let your desire and prayer be that the Lord will make you a blessing and a gift to everyone that comes your way. Make a commitment to always leave people better than you met them and to serve people in whatever capacity you can. This is the sign of true greatness.

The Lord Jesus Christ showed His disciples the greatest example of what being a true leader is, and it is by serving others. He said to them ...

> *But he that is greatest among you shall be your servant.*
>
> **(Matthew 23:11)**

He came to serve mankind through His sacrificial death on the cross of Calvary. Today, God has given Him a name that is above every other name.

> *Therefore God also has highly exalted Him and given Him the name which is above every name that at the name of Jesus every knee should bow, of those in heaven, and of those on earth, and of those under the earth, and that every tongue should confess that Jesus Christ is Lord, to the glory of God the Father.*
>
> **(Philippians 2:9-11)**

# CHAPTER SIXTEEN

# Live Life With The End In Mind

*"You will only be remembered for two things: the problems you solve or the ones you create"*

(Mike Murdoch)

A short while ago, as I was putting finishing touches to the first draft of this book, the world was mourning the departure of a great man called Evangelist Billy Graham. This was a man who had lived to be almost 100 years old and had preached the undiluted Word of God consistently for over 80 years of his life. By the time he died, he was said to have preached to millions of people all over the world and had also brought millions to salvation in Christ Jesus. He left behind a large family of 5 children, 19 grandchildren and about 44 great grandchildren and a ministry called The Billy Graham Evangelistic Association, that has outlived him.[1]

Many testimonies and messages filled various social media about the impact this man and his ministry had on the lives of people across different backgrounds and nations. A few days before his body was finally laid to rest, he was laid in honor at the United

States Capitol Rotunda in Washington, D.C. This is an event that is usually reserved for presidents and war heroes only. He was the fourth private citizen and the first religious leader to be so honored by the United States Government.

The following words were inscribed on his tombstone:

*** Billy Graham***
*** November 7, 1918- February 21, 2018***
*** Preacher of the Gospel of The Lord Jesus Christ***
*** John.14:6***

The above summarized the totality of what he lived and died for. He was passionate about soul winning and pursued this till he breathed his last.

Dear friend, what will be the summary of your life? What will be said about you by the time you leave this world? Whose life (or lives) would you have impacted? What problems would you have solved? Whose lives would you have brought joy to?

No one will ever live forever. Death is a debt we all owe. The prayer, however, is that when death comes, we will be ready to meet our Maker and that we will leave a good legacy behind. Therefore, we must be intentional and purposeful about the way we live our lives.

During my trainings on Personal Discovery, whenever I am leading a session on the topic, "Personal Vision and Goal Setting," I always ask the participants to do one thing. I ask them to begin to imagine they are at their 80th or 90th birthday party, surrounded by family members, friends, and well-wishers. I then ask them to write out the kinds of comments they would love to hear from each of these people as special tributes to them on that special day. Hardly have I come across anyone who expects to hear comments that are negative. We all would like to be celebrated and appreciated. However, being celebrated does not just happen overnight. It calls for consistent, persistent, and intentional sowing of the right kinds of seeds into the lives of others. It calls for living life purposefully, guided by a compelling mission and a vision.

Your mission is your calling, your purpose and your reason for being. It is the role you want to play in making the world a better place. As earlier mentioned, your calling (purpose) is tied to your **5Ps** and will always be the solution to a problem that will make the lives of others better. Your calling will be perfectly suited to your unique make-up and combination.

In the pursuit of purpose, it is always a good idea to come up with a Personal Mission Statement. This is simply a statement of your reason for being and your purpose. It will focus on who you want to become as a person and as said before, will be perfectly suited to your **5Ps.**

In coming up with your mission statement, I will suggest you try to answer the following questions …

1. **Whose life matters to me, the most?**
   (Look deep within you, to identify the group of people whose welfare is really uppermost in your life.)

   Examples of these are – Women, Rape victims, Abused, Abandoned, Widows, Children, Abandoned, Special needs, Students, Teenagers, Men, Elderly, the Physically and Mentally Challenged etc.)

   _____

   _____

2. **What would you like to do for these people?**
   (Every mission requires action. Therefore, you need to determine what exactly it is you would like to do for the selected group of people. Examples are: affect, inspire, educate, alleviate, encourage, create, reform etc.)

   _____

   _____

3. **What values would you like to pass across to this group of people?**
(Examples of values are Excellence, Integrity, Peace, Honesty, Joy, Dignity, Self-worth, Love etc.)

_____

_____

(Please note that the examples of target groups, action words and values listed above are not in any way exhaustive. There are so many others).

Now, having answered questions 1-3 above, you can now come up with a summarized version of your personal mission statement that should guide you all through life.

Below are some examples I came up with. My mission is …

➢ *"To communicate, promote and inspire self-worth and purposeful living in the lives of people, especially women."*
➢ *"To give every abandoned child the opportunity to be loved and cared for."*
➢ *"To write and publish books that will transform the lives of women and children."*
➢ *"To create and promote films that will enhance the dignity of every woman (or man)."*

Your life mission will also give birth to a vision. We will look at the subject of vision in the next chapter.

# CHAPTER SEVENTEEN

# Turn Your Vision Into Reality

*Where there is no vision, the people perish.*

**(Proverbs 29:18)**

A vision is simply a mental picture of a future that you desire. It is an image or an idea of your destination. Vision gives your life direction, focus and order. It gives you energy and the zeal to keep going. Having a vision also makes you get rid of distractions. It makes you know what to focus on, and where to direct your energy.

God is the originator of visions. A vision from God will solve problems; it will bless lives and transform society. Helen Keller, a woman, who at the age of eighteen months became deaf, dumb and blind once said that, ***"The only thing that is worse than being blind is having sight and no vision."*** [1]

These are very deep words, worthy of reflection, spoken by a woman who was visually impaired most of her life! The truth is that many people are merely looking, but very few can see beyond the ordinary. The Lord appeared to Abraham shortly after he had parted ways with Lot and said to him …

*Lift your eyes now and look from the place where you are—northward, southward, eastward, and westward; for all the land which you see I give to you and your descendants forever. And I will make your descendants as the dust of the earth; so that if a man could number the dust of the earth, then your descendants also could be numbered. Arise, walk in the land through its length and its width, for I give it to you.*

**(Genesis 15:14-17)**

God was simply challenging Abraham to expand his vision and see far and wide. It is interesting to note that God also told him that he could only access what he could see (or envision) with his eyes. The question, dear friend, is this ..., "What do you see?" What vision do you have for your life?

Your vision should stretch, inspire, and energize you. It should fill you with excitement each time you think about it. Do not just internalize the vision, but put it in writing. Write down the desired outcome you want, in various aspects of your life. It is important to have a vision for your life, your marriage (if married or when you get married), your family, your business, your ministry and so on.

The Lord told Habakkuk …

*Write the vision*
*And make it plain on tablets,*
*That he may run who reads it. For the vision is yet for an*
*appointed time;*
*But at the end it will speak, and it will not lie.*
*Though it tarries, wait for it;*
*Because it will surely come,*
*It will not tarry.*

**(Habakkuk 2:2-3)**

Putting things in writing gives you clarity. What you put in writing becomes your Vision Statement in that area of your life. It is a description of your desired outcome in every area of your life.

Below are some questions that can guide you to create your vision statement ...

1. **Where am I going?**

   _____

   _____

2. **What do I want to see when I get to my desired destination?**

   _____

   _____

3. **What picture do I have of my future concerning this particular area (career, marriage, family etc.) of my life?**

   _____

   _____

With your vision statement now clearly written out, the next step will be to begin to take steps to make the vision become a reality. It is one thing to have a vision; it is another thing to turn this vision into reality. When you do not take steps to make your vision become a reality, you are just daydreaming!

**How then do you turn vision into reality?**

1. The first thing is to set goals for yourself. Goals are milestones you want to achieve and should be set to cover various aspects of your life - Academic, Career, Family, Financial, Physical, Attitude, Spiritual parts of your life should be in line with your vision. Goals help you to translate your vision into reality. Goal setting is a powerful process that makes your vision a reality.

## Develop short, medium & long term goals for all aspects of your life...

— Spiritual
— Physical
— Financial
— Family
— Career

2. Set **SMART** Goals. SMART stands for Specific, Measurable, Achievable, Realistic and Time bound. In essence, goals must not be vague, but must be clearly spelt out in a way that makes them easy to evaluate, accomplish and must have a time frame attached to them.

   An example of a vague goal will be to say, "...This year, I must lose weight!" The question will be ...

   a. How much weight do you want to lose?
   b. What is the time frame?

   A better way to put it is, "By the end of this year, I want to lose 50 Ibs."

   Let us look at a few other examples ...

   a. **Financial goal**- By December of this year, I will have saved $6,000.
   c. **Spiritual goal**- By December of this year, I will have finished reading through the New Testament.
   d. **Academic goal**- In the next four years, I will have earned my college degree in nursing.

3. Now, after you have set the goals for various areas of your life, begin to develop daily, weekly, monthly, and yearly action plans. Planning is critical in life, as it helps you to remain focused and

get rid of distractions. The truth is this: If you fail to determine how you will spend your time, it creates room for time wasters to fill it up for you.

4. After taking out time to plan, begin to take specific steps to execute the plan. This calls for discipline and commitment on your part.

5. Engage the power of daily planning. This involves taking time out the night before, to plan for the activities of the next day. It is a great idea to have a clear picture of what you plan to do each day, if not, you will get distracted and will end up doing something you never planned for. You must be intentional about every day of your life. It is the little things that you accomplish each day that add up to create your success story. Launch out every day with great expectations and on a positive note.

Remember, the morning sets the tone for the rest of the day, so launch out well ...

# CHAPTER EIGHTEEN

# A Final Word
# It Begins and Ends with God

*Let us hear the conclusion of the whole matter:*
*"Fear God and keep His commandments, For*
*this is man's all.*

**(Ecclesiastes 12:13)**

I do hope and believe that you have been inspired and motivated by the contents of this book. My desire is that you have been better informed and educated about your purpose and calling in life.

I would however like to share a particularly important message with you as you read this concluding chapter. You see, one can apply all the principles listed out in this book and achieve great and outstanding results in life. However, there is something much more important than merely setting goals and achieving them. That is the need to have the assurance that at the end of it all, after all the fame and the success, one has the assurance of making it to Heaven. There is a destination for us all when we leave this earth and drop our earthly casing. The choices we make here on earth will determine where we will end up when we die - either Heaven or Hell.

However, it is not God's desire that anyone of us should miss Heaven. That was why He sent the Lord Jesus Christ to die for you and me on the cross of Calvary.

*For God so loved the world that He gave His only begotten Son, that whoever believes in Him should not perish but have everlasting life.*

**(John3:16)**

Jesus paid the ultimate price for our sins and declared as He gave up the ghost on the cross, "It is finished." Everything that is needed to be done for us to have eternal life and a place in Heaven has already been finished. All we need do now is just to ask God for His forgiveness and receive The Lord Jesus Christ into our lives as our Lord and Savior.

Therefore, if you would like to receive God's forgiveness and invite the Lord Jesus Christ into your heart as your Lord and Savior, please say this prayer after me now ...

*"Father, I thank You for Your mercy and love towards me,*
*Please have mercy upon me and forgive me for all my sins.*
*Cleanse me Lord, with the precious blood of Your Son, Jesus.*
*Lord Jesus, I invite you into my heart as*
*my personal Lord and Savior.*
*Please give me the grace to serve You for the*
*rest of my life, in Jesus' mighty name.*
*Thank You, Lord.*
*Amen."*

If you said this prayer in sincerity of heart, I congratulate you for this wonderful decision. You have just commenced the most exciting journey of your life. I encourage you now to locate a good

Bible-believing church where you can worship and begin to grow as a Christian.

Also, get an easy-to-understand Bible version and begin to read it every day. God speaks to us through the pages of the Bible. Most of all, I want you to begin to talk to God confidently, beginning from today. He is now your Father, and you are His child. Welcome to the family of God!

If you have any questions on your newfound faith, you can also contact the author by sending an email to Koredefasoro@gmail.com or visit www.newbelieverinchrist.life

# REFERENCES

**Chapter Two**

1  Rick Warren, *The Purpose Driven Life*, (Michigan, Zondervan, 2012)
2  https://en.wikipedia.org/wiki/The_Purpose_Driven_Life
3  Mike Murdoch, *The Assignment*, (Oklahoma, Albury Publishing, 1997)

**Chapter Three**

1  Joyce Meyer, *The Confident Woman, (New York, Faith Works, 2010),* Page 18
2  Pat Harrison, *Woman, Wife and Mother (Oklahoma, Harrison House Inc 1984) Pages 10 & 11*
3  https://quotefancy.com/quote/1537537/Myles-Munroe-When-purpose-is-not-known-abuse-is-inevitable

**Chapter Four**

1  Susan Nolen- Hoeksema. *The Power of Women* (New York, Times Books, 2010) Pages 1&2

**Chapter Six**

1  Rick Warren, *The Purpose Driven Life* (Michigan, Zondervan, 2012), Page 27
2  Max Lucado, *Cure for the Common Life* (Tennesse, Thomas Nelson, 2005) Page 1
3  Rick Warren, *Purpose Driven Life* (Michigan, Zondervan, 2012), Page 26
4  https://www.oxfordlearnersdictionaries.com/us/definition/american_english/masterpiece#
5  https://www.merriam-webster.com/dictionary/masterpiece

6    Rick Warren, *Purpose Driven life* (Michigan, Zondervan, 2012), Page 239-246

7    Max Lucado, *Cure for the Common Life* (Tennesse, Thomas Nelson, 2005) Page1

## Chapter Seven

1    https://www.youtube.com/watch?v=1lfLpmYz7RQ - Teaching by Doctor Myles Munroe on The Potential Principle by Munroe Global

## Chapter Eight

1    Nick Vujicic (voo-yi-chich) is an Australian-American born without arms or legs who has become a world-renowned speaker, New York Times best-selling author, coach and entrepreneur. https://nickvujicic.com/

2    https://youtu.be/tJnJ_fTYofQ - Interview with Nick Vujicic on 60mins - Australia

## Chapter Nine

1    Florence Littauer, *Personality Plus* (Michigan, Fleming H. Revell, 1993) Page 3

2    https://dictionary.cambridge.org/us/dictionary/english/personality

## Chapter Ten

1    https://www.womenshistory.org/education-resources/biographies/florence-nightingale

2    http://maryslessor.org/mary-slessor/

3    http://www.harriettubmanbiography.com/harriet-tubman-biography.html

## Chapter Eleven

1    Myles Munroe, Understanding Your Potential, (Shippensburg PA,1991) Page 21

2    https://www.brainyquote.com/quotes/thomas_guthrie_197202

## Chapter Fourteen

1    https://www.success.com/15-quotes-to-overcome-your-self-limiting-beliefs/

**Chapter Fifteen**

1    https://www.nobelprize.org/prizes/peace/1979/teresa/biographical/

**Chapter Sixteen**

1    https://billygraham.org/about/biographies/billy-graham/

**Chapter Seventeen**

1    https://www.brainyquote.com/quotes/helen_keller_383771

# ABOUT THE AUTHOR

Omokorede is a passionate and anointed teacher of the Word, a certified trainer, writer, speaker, and personal discovery coach. She has close to 20 years' experience as a professional trainer in various capacities and at different levels, most especially in the areas of personal discovery, self-development, and entrepreneurship.

She holds a BSc. in quantity surveying, an MSc. in media and communication from the Pan Atlantic University in Lagos Nigeria, and a PGCE (international) from the University of Nottingham, United Kingdom. She is an ILO (International Labor Organization) certified trainer in the Gender and Enterprise Development (GET Ahead) and Financial Education and has also been trained by the ILO in the Start and Improve Your Business (SIYB) and Expand Your Business (EYB) training modules. She also holds certifications as a Job Skills Trainer/Coach and Job Placement specialist from the University of North Texas (WISE) program.

Mrs. Fasoro is the founder and coordinator of the Women of Essence Foundation- a non-profit organization which she established about nine years ago in Lagos, Nigeria. This foundation was born out of her personal experience, which she refers to as her "wilderness season," when she battled with depression and low self-esteem, all in the search for purpose and relevance. The organization has the mission to help women discover, pursue and fulfil their God ordained purpose, through training, counseling, mentoring and empowerment of women and young ladies.

In 2019, she started the Mary Group - a weekly online Bible study & prayer group - for women from various nations and across diverse backgrounds. Through the Mary Group, she teaches and mentors women who are eager to have a deeper relationship with God, as recorded in Luke 10:42.

She is an ordained assistant pastor at the Redeemed Christian Church of God, where she and her husband have been serving for over 20 years. Omokorede is happily married to Ayotunde her husband of 27 years, and they are blessed with what she refers to as two generations of wonderful children.

To find out more about the author and her various training, coaching and mentoring programs, and other books authored by her, please visit her website at **www.omokoredefasoro.net** or connect with her on Twitter: Twitter.com/Kfasoro